A Cure for the Common WORD

K.D. Sullivan

McGraw Hill

New York Chicago San Francisco Lisbon London Madrid Mexico City
Milan New Delhi San Juan Seoul Singapore Sydney Toronto

Library of Congress Cataloging-in-Publication Data

Sullivan, K.D.
    A cure for the common word : remedy your ailing vocabulary with 3,000+ vibrant alternatives to the most overused words / by K.D. Sullivan.
        p.   cm.
     ISBN 0-07-149330-1 (alk. paper)
     1. Vocabulary.   2. English language—Glossaries, vocabularies, etc.   I. Title.

PE1449.S85   2007
428.1—dc22   2007016928

I want to thank my mom, Ann Longknife, Ph.D., for planting the seed of a book on vocabulary building. As a teacher of English and critical thinking at the College of San Mateo, she sees her students struggling with broadening their understanding of new words, and I hope this book will be helpful. And a huge thank-you to Karen Young, acquisitions editor—and so much more—at McGraw-Hill, who with her inspiration, creativity, encouragement, and kindness has guided me through every step of the creation of this book. Thank-you to Craig Bolt, who has so expertly shepherded the editing and production of this book.

1 2 3 4 5 6 7 8 9 10 11 12 13 14 15 16 17 18 19 20 21   FGR/FGR   0 9 8 7

ISBN   978-0-07-149330-7
MHID   0-07-149330-1

Interior design by Village Typographers, Inc.

McGraw-Hill books are available at special quantity discounts to use as premiums and sales promotions, or for use in corporate training programs. For more information, please write to the Director of Special Sales, Professional Publishing, McGraw-Hill, Two Penn Plaza, New York, NY 10121-2298. Or contact your local bookstore.

This book is printed on acid-free paper.

Contents

1 Introduction

6 **absolutely** ADVERB

8 **activity** NOUN

10 **affect** VERB

12 **amazing** ADJECTIVE

14 **awesome** ADJECTIVE

16 **bad** ADJECTIVE

18 **basic** ADJECTIVE

20 **beautiful** ADJECTIVE

22 **begin** VERB

24 **better** ADJECTIVE

26 **big** ADJECTIVE

28 **boring** ADJECTIVE

30 **bring** VERB

32 **certain** ADJECTIVE

34 **change** VERB

36 **choose** VERB

38 **common** ADJECTIVE

40 **correct** ADJECTIVE

42 **correct** VERB

44 **decent** ADJECTIVE

46 **develop** VERB

48 **difficult** ADJECTIVE

50 **difficult** ADJECTIVE

52 **direct** ADJECTIVE

54 **do** VERB

56 **easy** ADJECTIVE

58 **effective** ADJECTIVE

60 **emphasize** VERB

62 **end** VERB

64 **energy** NOUN

66 **enjoy** VERB

68 **enough** ADJECTIVE

70 **excellent** ADJECTIVE

72 **exciting** ADJECTIVE

74 **fast** ADJECTIVE

76 **feel** VERB

78 **fill** VERB

80 **final** ADJECTIVE

82 **fine** ADJECTIVE

84 **finish** VERB

86 **funny** ADJECTIVE

88 **get** VERB

90 **give** VERB

92 **go** VERB

94 **good** ADJECTIVE

96 **good** ADJECTIVE

98 **great** ADJECTIVE

100 **grow** VERB

102 **happy** ADJECTIVE

104 **hard** ADJECTIVE

106 **help** VERB

108 **important** ADJECTIVE

110 **interesting** ADJECTIVE

112 **keep** VERB

114 **kind** ADJECTIVE

116 **know** VERB

118 **leave** VERB

120 **look** NOUN

122 **love** NOUN

124 **main** ADJECTIVE

126 **make** VERB

128 **mean** ADJECTIVE

130 **more** ADJECTIVE

132 **need** NOUN

134 **new** ADJECTIVE

136 **next** ADJECTIVE

138 **nice** ADJECTIVE

140 **old** ADJECTIVE

142 **old** ADJECTIVE

144 **open** ADJECTIVE

146 **part** NOUN

148 **perfect** ADJECTIVE

150 **piece** NOUN

152 **plain** ADJECTIVE

154 **plan** NOUN

156 **plan** VERB

158 **pleasant** ADJECTIVE

160 **problem** NOUN

162 **prove** VERB

164 **put** VERB

166 **quick** ADJECTIVE

168 **quick** ADJECTIVE

170 **ready** ADJECTIVE

172 **regular** ADJECTIVE

174 **short** ADJECTIVE

176 **simple** ADJECTIVE

178 **small** ADJECTIVE

180 **special** ADJECTIVE

182 **stay** VERB

184 **strange** ADJECTIVE

186 **take** VERB

188 **take** VERB

190 **thin** ADJECTIVE

192 **think** VERB

194 **try** VERB

196 **use** VERB

198 **usual** ADJECTIVE

200 **want** VERB

202 **weird** ADJECTIVE

204 **well** ADVERB

206 Minicapsules

Introduction

I'm reading a very interesting book.

Can you tell from the preceding sentence exactly what I mean by *interesting*? Not really. But what if I say, "I'm reading a very *helpful* book" or "I'm reading a very *comprehensive* book"? By changing just one word in this sentence to a more specific word, I convey a different meaning and give you more information about what I want to say. That's the goal of *A Cure for the Common Word*—to help you learn to more precisely convey your intended meaning when you write and when you speak.

Many of us tend to use the same words over and over. Even though it is estimated that the average person knows more than twenty thousand words, he or she uses only about 10 percent of those in daily life. Often it's out of habit or because it's easier to use the same old words, but sometimes it's because we don't fully understand the nuance of some alternative words or when it might be appropriate—and more powerful—to use them.

Granted, sometimes a vague or ambiguous word is just what you want—for example, when you are being discreet or want to leave your words open to interpretation. For example, if friends set you up on a less-than-stellar blind date, you can gracefully get out of giving a negative opinion by vaguely describing your date as a "nice" guy.

If you do want to be specific, then by expanding your repertoire of words, when you write and speak you will be able to use the most precise word for your meaning, not just the first word that comes to mind. And by using these more precise words, you will be able to communicate *exactly* what you mean and will do so in a quick and concise manner.

Using the same example of our blind date—and assuming this time that the date with Rich was a positive one—see what happens when we use different alternatives for our "nice" guy?

Rich has a nice personality.

Substitute an alternative remedy for *nice*:

Rich has a(n) _____ personality.

cordial   Rich is warm, sincere, and friendly.

cultured   Rich is refined in his manner and enlightened and knowledgeable in the arts.

gentle   Rich is never severe or harsh in any way.

gracious   Rich is kind and courteous and has a compassionate nature.

A Cure for the Common Word is for anyone from middle-school age to adult, for those who write and speak in their profession and those eager to improve their vocabulary to be more effective in what they say.

For example, did you know that in the preceding sentence, *eager* is exactly the right word, rather than *anxious*, which many people would have used? That's because *eager* means having or showing keen interest or intense desire, whereas *anxious* means uneasy and apprehensive about an uncertain event.

How to Use This Book

This book includes one hundred of the most commonly overused words in the English language, based on research from several sources. Because these common words can often be vague, limiting, or confusing in a sentence, we'll show you how choosing specific alternatives to these common words helps you to more precisely convey your intended meaning.

Before we describe the elements of this book, let's take a brief look at the definitions of a few terms used throughout the book:

connotation—the associated or secondary meaning of a word or an expression in addition to its explicit or primary meaning

definition—a statement of the meaning of a word, phrase, or term, as in a dictionary entry

impression—a strong effect produced on the intellect, feelings, conscience, etc.

meaning—what is intended to be, or actually is, expressed or indicated

nuance—a subtle difference or distinction in expression, meaning, response, etc.

Each of these refers to going beyond the definition of a word, to the subtleties of what you mean—or what is perceived.

Now a guide to help you with the symptoms of and cures for the common words in this book.

A number of elements are associated with each of the one hundred common words in this book. The following descriptions will help you gain the most use of the alternatives offered in this book.

On each left-hand page, you'll see

- **The common word.** Be alert because of the one hundred common words, a few are the same word in spelling but not in definition. You're not seeing double.

- **The common word's part of speech.**

- **A brief definition or definitions of the common word.** Some common words are given only one definition, but other common words can be defined more than one way, all similar in nature.

- **Seven alternatives to the common word.** The meanings of these will all appear on the right-hand page.

- **A more thorough list of alternatives for the common word.** Though this list may not include all synonyms, we've listed the most relevant and/or powerful alternatives. A traditional thesaurus—in print or online—may list more words in all their forms, including their parts of speech.

- **And for fun, a famous quote.** The quote gives an example in which one of the alternatives was just the right word—the precise cure for what the speaker wanted to say.

On each right-hand page, you'll find

- **The diagnosis.** Each of the common words has some symptoms that need a cure. The diagnosis of the problem will be *vague*, *limiting*, or *confusing*.

- **A sentence using the common word.** Think of this as our "patient." Here's where you'll see how the common word may not convey clearly what you want to say (vague), doesn't say enough of what you'd like to convey (limiting), or could have different meanings (confusing).

- **The sentence's meaning.** Here are the "symptoms" of the common word—what the sentence means as written and how using the common word may keep us from understanding what's truly meant.

- **Expanded alternatives and meanings.** These "remedies" to our diagnosis are just a few of the many options you can choose from to highlight a primary point you want to make or a meaning you want to imply. Note that these alternative meanings and explanations are not definitions. Some alternatives are very similar and offer only slight nuances—subtle connotations or implications that evoke slightly different feelings or perceptions of what's meant. Others show how changing the word can dramatically change the actual meaning of the sentence. So look for key words to differentiate the implications of using each alternative.

- **A second quote.** Another fun, inspirational, or witty quote illustrates how choosing one of the alternative words gives a sentence—or sentiment—power and precise meaning.

A Wealth of Words

Because English has welcomed influences from so many other languages, you have a wealth of word choices to consider. Here are a few statistics you may not be aware of:

- The English language consists of more than a million words, if you include technical and scientific terms.

- The *Oxford English Dictionary* (*OED*), Second Edition, contains approximately 291,500 main entries with a total of more than 600,000 definitions, and *Merriam-Webster's Collegiate Dictionary*, Eleventh Edition, contains approximately 25,000 main entries and more than 400,000 definitions!

- Experts estimate that the average educated person knows about 20,000 words and uses about 2,000 in a week.

It's actually pretty great that we have so many ways to express ourselves, and it can be fun discovering and using just the right word to say so precisely/exactly/perfectly/ideally/eloquently what we want to say/express/convey/write/communicate.

One of the very best ways that you can improve your vocabulary and develop your writing and speaking skills is to read, read, read. As you do, be aware of how effective writers present their ideas in ways that enable you to know and feel exactly what they're saying, as if you're right in the middle of the action.

I hope that the examples and alternatives to the common words in this book give you a great deal of information of what's possible. And I hope that this is a springboard for you to try new words, not only with the common overused words in this book, but in all your writing and speaking.

This book is for all those who are eternally curious, who have a joy in learning, and who ask and seek when they don't know.

Have fun!

absolutely

PART OF SPEECH	*adverb*
DEFINITION	*positively; certainly; having no restriction, exception, or qualification*

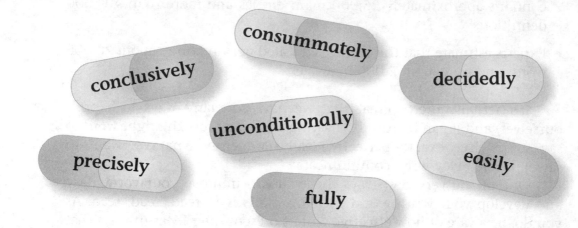

cures for the common word

actually	**easily**	straight out
categorically	entirely	sure enough
completely	exactly	surely
conclusively	**fully**	thoroughly
consummately	ideally	truly
decidedly	positively	unambiguously
decisively	**precisely**	**unconditionally**
def	purely	unquestionably
definitely	really	utterly
doubtless	right on	wholly

*Frodo: "You're late." Gandalf: "A wizard is never late, Frodo Baggins. Nor is he early. He arrives **precisely** when he means to."*

J. R. R. TOLKIEN

Bob is **absolutely** the right person for the job.

We know from this sentence that Bob is a good choice, but we'd like more information on how that was determined or why he is so right for the job.

powerful remedies

Substitute an alternative remedy for *absolutely*:

Bob is _____ the right person for the job.

conclusively	There were some questions as to whether Bob was right for the job, and this puts an end to any debate.
consummately	Bob has the highest degree of qualifications for the job.
decidedly	There was never any hesitation that Bob was right for the job.
easily	Neither discussion nor considering other candidates was even necessary, because Bob is without question right for the job.
fully	Bob is right for the job in every manner and degree.
precisely	For some or many reasons, Bob is exactly the right choice—even if he doesn't match an original profile of who would be right.
unconditionally	Bob is right for the job, with no conditions or limits on that perspective.

CURED!

*Effort only **fully** releases its reward after a person refuses to quit.*

NAPOLEON HILL

activity

PART OF SPEECH	*noun*
DEFINITION	*a specific deed, action, or function*

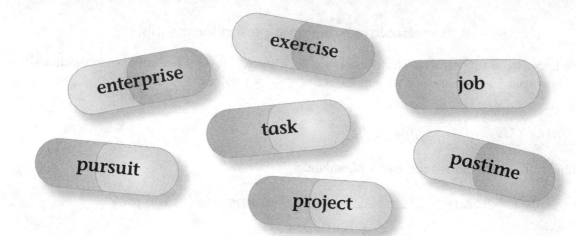

cures for the common word

act	**exercise**	**pursuit**
avocation	game	racket
bag	hobby	scene
ball game	interest	scheme
bit	**job**	stunt
deed	labor	**task**
endeavor	occupation	undertaking
enterprise	**pastime**	venture
entertainment	**project**	work

*There are some **enterprises** in which a careful disorderliness is the true method.*

HERMAN MELVILLE

Matt stayed after school to spend time on his **activity**.

We're unsure whether Matt is spending time on something fun—or not fun. The following alternatives give us more information.

powerful remedies

Substitute an alternative remedy for *activity*:

Matt stayed after school to spend time on his _____.

enterprise	Matt is doing something that involves his ingenuity or is related to something entrepreneurial.
exercise	Matt is doing something as a means of practice or training.
job	Matt is performing work as part of the routine of his occupation, possibly for pay.
pastime	Matt is enjoying a hobby or something that amuses him.
project	Matt is working on something he has contemplated or devised either for fun or to meet an obligation, such as a science project.
pursuit	Matt is putting in an effort to attain something that meets special criteria for him, a quest, such as practicing and honing a particular skill.
task	Matt has a commonly assigned piece of work to be finished within a certain time.

CURED!

*Defining and analyzing humor is a **pastime** of humorless people.*
ROBERT BENCHLEY

affect

PART OF SPEECH	*verb*
DEFINITION	*to produce a material influence upon or alteration in*

influence

alter

modify

upset

transform

prompt

sway

cures for the common word

act on	inspire	prevail
alter	interest	**prompt**
change	involve	regard
disturb	moderate	relate
impinge	**modify**	stir
impress	motivate	**sway**
incline	move	touch
induce	overcome	**transform**
influence	perturb	**upset**

CURED!

*Some painters **transform** the sun into a yellow spot, others transform a yellow spot into the sun.*

PABLO PICASSO

Your decision will **affect** the outcome.

We know the outcome will be altered, but not how much your decision will be an influence, or if it will be positive or negative or to your advantage or the advantage of others.

Substitute an alternative remedy for *affect*:

Your decision will _____ the outcome.

alter
The outcome will be different in some ways, but without completely changing it into something new.

influence
You have the power or capacity to cause a change in indirect or intangible ways—presumably in your favor—and this may indicate negative interference.

modify
Your decision will cause fundamental changes to the outcome and may even give a new orientation to the end.

prompt
Your decision will spur on action.

sway
Your decision will have a controlling influence, possibly in a way that benefits you but not necessarily others.

transform
Your decision will greatly change the outcome in a positive way.

upset
Your decision will unexpectedly defeat an anticipated outcome.

CURED!

We write frankly and freely but then we "modify" before we print.

MARK TWAIN

amazing

PART OF SPEECH *adjective*
DEFINITION *causing great surprise or sudden wonder*

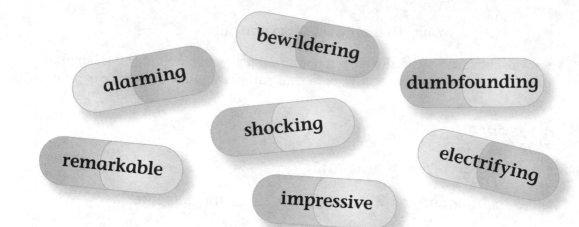

cures for the common word

affecting	dazzling	**remarkable**
alarming	**dumbfounding**	**shocking**
astonishing	**electrifying**	staggering
astounding	flabbergasting	startling
bewildering	**impressive**	striking
blown away	moving	stunning
bowled down	overwhelming	stupefying
bowled over	perplexing	touching
dazing	put away	unexpected

*Love is the only **shocking** act left on the face of the earth.*

SANDRA BERNHARD

The magician performed **amazing** tricks.

We were all amazed at the wonder of the magician's tricks, but *amazing* doesn't specify whether the experience was intellectual or emotional, positive or negative. There are different ways to be amazed.

powerful remedies

Substitute an alternative remedy for *amazing*:

The magician performed _____ tricks.

alarming	The tricks were startling and caused a sudden fear or panic.
bewildering	The tricks confused us, especially because of their complexity, variety, and multitude of objects and considerations.
dumbfounding	The tricks were so remarkable that we didn't know what to say.
electrifying	The tricks startled us and thrilled us.
impressive	The tricks made such an impression on us that we marveled at how the magician was able to accomplish them.
remarkable	The tricks were uncommon in an extraordinary way.
shocking	The tricks were extremely startling, distressing, or offensive.

*I deny the lawfulness of telling a lie to a sick man for fear of **alarming** him. You have no business with consequences; you are to tell the truth.*

SAMUEL JOHNSON

awesome

PART OF SPEECH	adjective
DEFINITION	very impressive; inspiring; terrific, extraordinary

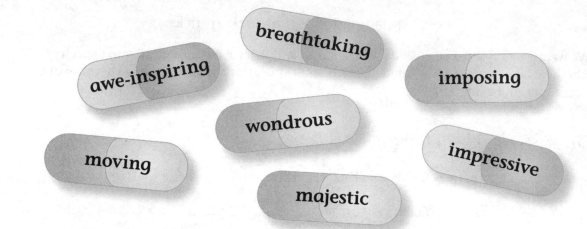

awe-inspiring
breathtaking
imposing
wondrous
moving
impressive
majestic

cures for the common word

alarming	formidable	nervous
astonishing	frantic	outstanding
awe-inspiring	frightening	overwhelming
awful	grand	shocking
beautiful	horrifying	striking
breathtaking	**imposing**	stunning
daunting	**impressive**	stupefying
dreadful	intimidating	stupendous
exalted	magnificent	terrible
fabulous	**majestic**	terrifying
fearful	mind-blowing	wonderful
fearsome	**moving**	**wondrous**

CURED!

*Thunder is good, thunder is **impressive**; but it is lightning that does the work.*
MARK TWAIN

The view of Bryce Canyon's rock formations was **awesome**.

Awesome is an all-encompassing description of the rock formations, which made a significant impression on us, but limits us from knowing just how the view impacted us.

powerful remedies

Substitute an alternative remedy for *awesome*:

The view of Bryce Canyon's rock formations was _____.

awe-inspiring	The view inspired awe by its exceptional beauty.
breathtaking	The view was exciting, thrilling, and astonishing, figuratively taking our breath away, because we'd never seen anything like this before.
imposing	The formations were very impressive because of their great size, dignity, and stately appearance.
impressive	The view gave us a feeling of respect and admiration for what nature had created.
majestic	The view had an air of authority and dignity—superior to mundane matters.
moving	The view was stirring and evoked strong feelings or emotions.
wondrous	The view is to be marveled at, and we appreciated its wonder, uniqueness, or other special qualities.

*The speed of communications is **wondrous** to behold. It is also true that speed can multiply the distribution of information that we know to be untrue.*

EDWARD R. MURROW

bad

PART OF SPEECH   *adjective*
DEFINITION   *of poor or inferior quality; defective; deficient*

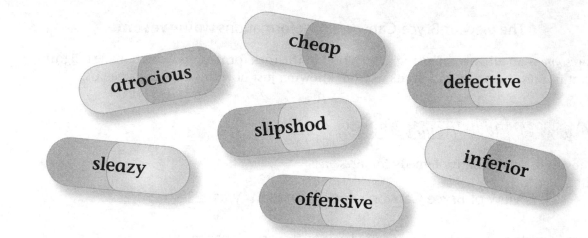

cures for the common word

abominable	disagreeable	**offensive**
amiss	dissatisfactory	poor
atrocious	dreadful	repulsive
awful	erroneous	rough
bad news	fallacious	sad
beastly	faulty	skuzzy
bottom out	harmful	**sleazy**
bummer	imperfect	**slipshod**
careless	inadequate	stinking
cheap	incorrect	substandard
corrupt	**inferior**	synthetic
crummy	injurious	unacceptable
defective	lousy	unfavorable
deficient	off	unsatisfactory

CURED!

*You'd be surprised how much it costs to look this **cheap**.*

DOLLY PARTON

> One of the judges felt the contestant's **bad** costume ruined
> the performance.

Using *bad* doesn't indicate what the judge thought was so awful about the costume, and the alternatives tell us more about how the quality of a costume could ruin a whole performance.

powerful remedies

Substitute an alternative remedy for *bad*:

> One of the judges felt the contestant's _____ costume ruined
> the performance.

atrocious
The contestant's costume was shockingly dreadful, abominable—extremely awful.

cheap
Nothing negative about something being inexpensive, but *cheap* gives the implication that it is also of poor quality.

defective
The costume wasn't working properly during the performance.

inferior
The contestant's costume didn't meet high enough expectations to make a good impression.

offensive
The contestant's costume was disagreeable and repugnant to the senses, morally or otherwise.

sleazy
The costume was flimsy, and the connotation is that it didn't show the class or sophistication it probably should have.

slipshod
The costume was sloppy, and the judge could tell it was put together carelessly.

CURED!

*Revenge is not always sweet, once it is consummated we feel **inferior** to our victim.*

EMILE M. CIORAN

basic

PART OF SPEECH   *adjective*
DEFINITION   *elementary; of, being, or serving as a starting point; fundamental*

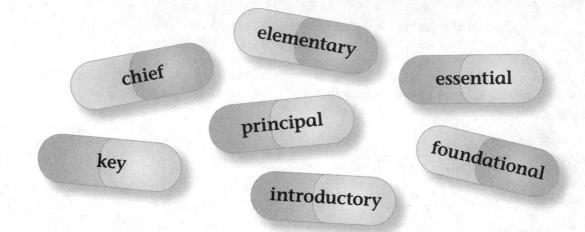

cures for the common word

basal	**foundational**	primary
beginning	fundamental	primitive
capital	indispensable	**principal**
central	inherent	radical
chief	intrinsic	rudimentary
easy	**introductory**	simplified
elemental	**key**	substratal
elementary	main	underlying
essential	necessary	vital

> In the television age, the **key** distinction is between the candidate who can speak poetry and the one who can only speak prose.
>
> RICHARD M. NIXON

Our textbook covered the **basic** concepts of advertising.

We can tell that the concepts in the book are necessary in any study of advertising, but the definition of what is considered *basic* isn't clear.

powerful remedies

Substitute an alternative remedy for *basic*:

Our textbook covered the _____ concepts of advertising.

chief	These are the most important concepts, though there are different perspectives on what is most important.
elementary	The concepts covered pertain to the rudimentary principles of advertising.
essential	The concepts covered are indispensable and should not be disregarded.
foundational	These concepts represent the groundwork on which more advanced study will be based.
introductory	The concepts covered serve as only a starting point, with much more to be learned.
key	The major and pivotal concepts are covered; *key* may also mean the concepts are presented in a brief or condensed manner.
principal	Concepts of highest importance are covered.

CURED!

*All men who have turned out worth anything have had the **chief** hand in their own education.*

SIR WALTER SCOTT

beautiful

PART OF SPEECH	*adjective*
DEFINITION	*having qualities that give great pleasure or satisfaction to the senses or mind*

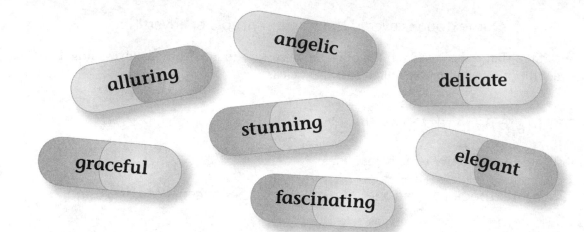

cures for the common word

alluring	enticing	marvelous
angelic	excellent	pleasing
appealing	exquisite	pretty
attractive	fair	radiant
beauteous	**fascinating**	ravishing
bewitching	fine	refined
charming	foxy	resplendent
classy	good-looking	shapely
comely	gorgeous	splendid
cute	**graceful**	statuesque
dazzling	grand	**stunning**
delicate	handsome	sublime
delightful	ideal	superb
divine	lovely	taking
elegant	magnificent	wonderful

*To love for the sake of being loved is human, but to love for the sake of loving is **angelic**.*

ALPHONSE DE LEMARTINE

The **beautiful** statue caught our attention.

We know the statue is appealing and attention grabbing, but we're not sure exactly in what way.

powerful remedies

Substitute an alternative remedy for *beautiful*:

The _____ statue caught our attention.

alluring	The statue has a tempting, enticing, or seductive quality.
angelic	The statue is befitting an angel, especially in beauty or in expressing virtue.
delicate	The details or craftsmanship of the statue is exquisitely fine or dainty.
elegant	The statue is luxurious in style or design.
fascinating	There's something about the look or meaning of the statue that is of great interest or attraction.
graceful	The statue is pleasing or attractive in line, proportion, or movement.
stunning	The statue is strikingly impressive, especially in beauty or excellence.

*Grow **graceful**, growing old.*

ANONYMOUS

begin

PART OF SPEECH	*verb*
DEFINITION	*to perform the first or earliest part of some action; to commence; to start*

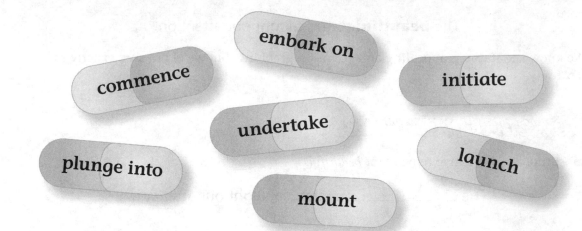

cures for the common word

activate	generate	make
actualize	get going	make active
break ground	give impulse	motivate
bring about	go ahead	**mount**
cause	go into	occasion
commence	impel	open
create	inaugurate	originate
effect	induce	**plunge into**
embark on	**initiate**	prepare
enter on	instigate	produce
enter upon	institute	set about
establish	introduce	set up
eventuate	**launch**	trigger
found	lead	**undertake**

*Two of the most difficult tasks a writer can **undertake**, to write the truth about himself and about his mother.*

TIME MAGAZINE

The military will **begin** the offensive in twenty-four hours.

The use of *begin* tells us when the action will start, but it doesn't give us a clear idea of the military's role and intent.

powerful remedies

Substitute an alternative remedy for *begin*:

The military will _____ the offensive in twenty-four hours.

commence	The military is taking the first step to set the offensive in motion.
embark on	The military is about to begin a major offensive.
initiate	The military will take the lead in the offensive.
launch	The military will enter enthusiastically into the offensive.
mount	The military will be increasing the amount or intensity of the offensive.
plunge into	The military will forcibly thrust into the offensive, or perhaps it is moving ahead suddenly.
undertake	The military is taking it upon itself to achieve its objective.

*Courage is the ladder on which all the other virtues **mount**.*

CLARE BOOTHE LUCE

better

PART OF SPEECH	*adjective*
DEFINITION	*greater in excellence or higher in quality*

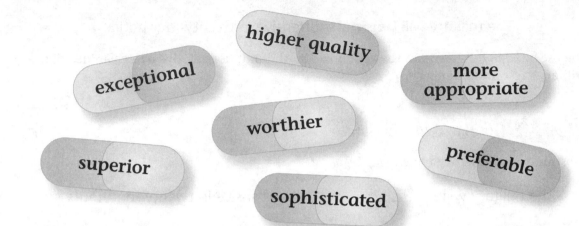

higher quality

exceptional

more appropriate

worthier

superior

preferable

sophisticated

cures for the common word

bigger
choice
exceeding
exceptional
finer
fitter
greater
higher quality

improved
larger
more appropriate
more desirable
more fitting
more select
more suitable
more useful

more valuable
preferable
preferred
prominent
sophisticated
superior
surpassing
worthier

CURED!

*The qualities of an **exceptional** cook are akin to those of a successful tight-rope walker: an abiding passion for the task, courage to go out on a limb and an impeccable sense of balance.*

BRYAN MILLER

George is a **better** choice for lead guitarist.

We'd like to know what particular quality makes George the better choice and why better than someone else.

powerful remedies

Substitute an alternative remedy for *better*:

George is a _____ choice for lead guitarist.

exceptional	George is an unusually excellent lead guitarist, making him one of a select, exclusive group.
higher quality	George's talents are above those of others who were compared.
more appropriate	George is the better choice for reasons beyond his playing skills; for example, he may look better for the part or have good connections in the industry.
preferable	George is the choice over others, but *preferable* still doesn't tell us exactly why.
sophisticated	George's music appeals to the tastes of a more discerning or knowledgeable audience.
superior	George's talents are above those of the average guitarist.
worthier	George is more deserving of the gig of lead guitarist.

*The risk of a wrong decision is **preferable** to the terror of indecision.*

MAIMONIDES

big

PART OF SPEECH — *adjective*
DEFINITION — *large, as in size, height, width, or amount*

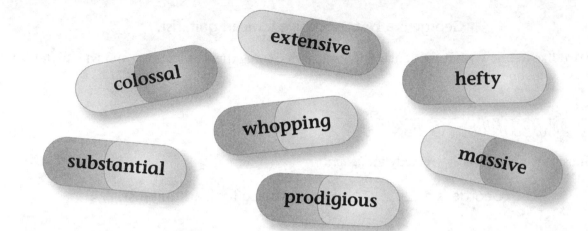

cures for the common word

ample	gigantic	oversize
brimming	heavy-duty	ponderous
bulky	heavyweight	**prodigious**
burly	**hefty**	roomy
capacious	huge	sizable
chock-full	hulking	spacious
colossal	humungous	strapping
commodious	husky	stuffed
considerable	immense	**substantial**
copious	jumbo	thundering
enormous	king-sized	vast
extensive	mammoth	voluminous
fat	**massive**	walloping
full	monster	**whopping**

CURED!

*Old age is like climbing a mountain. You climb from ledge to ledge. The higher you get, the more tired and breathless you become, but your views become more **extensive**.*

INGMAR BERGMAN

Casey stood beside the **big** marble columns of the Acropolis.

We all have different perspectives on size, and *big* in this sentence doesn't give us a familiar frame of reference, whereas some of the alternatives give us a much better sense of the columns' enormity.

powerful remedies

Substitute an alternative remedy for *big*:

Casey stood beside the _____ marble columns of the Acropolis.

colossal	Generally meaning "extraordinarily great in size," in architecture *colossal* can also pertain to a classical order whose columns span two or more stories of a building.
extensive	The columns extend over a great area.
hefty	The columns are clearly heavy and weighty.
massive	The columns are large and bulky.
prodigious	Many things can be big, but *prodigious* gives the sense that to you they are unusually great in size.
substantial	Not only are the columns big in size, but they are also of solid and strong construction.
whopping	An informal way to say, "Those columns are huge!"

CURED!

*Why does a slight tax increase cost you two hundred dollars and a **substantial** tax cut save you thirty cents?*

PEG BRACKEN

boring

PART OF SPEECH	*adjective*
DEFINITION	*uninteresting and tiresome; dull*

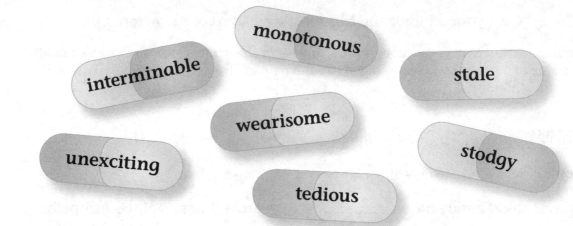

cures for the common word

bomb	**interminable**	stuffy
bromidic	irksome	stupid
characterless	lifeless	tame
colorless	**monotonous**	**tedious**
commonplace	platitudinous	threadbare
drab	plebeian	tiresome
drag	prosaic	tiring
drudging	repetitious	trite
dull	routine	**unexciting**
flat	spiritless	vapid
ho-hum	**stale**	**wearisome**
humdrum	stereotypical	well-worn
insipid	**stodgy**	zero

*Poetry is like fish: if it's fresh, it's good; if it's **stale**, it's bad; and if you're not certain, try it on the cat.*

OSBERT SITWELL

Michael and Beth sat through a **boring** movie.

From this sentence, it's likely a safe bet that Michael and Beth didn't enjoy the movie, but we don't know what specific qualities made it so dull.

powerful remedies

Substitute an alternative remedy for *boring*:

Michael and Beth sat through a _____ movie.

interminable	The movie was so monotonously or annoyingly long that they thought it would never end.
monotonous	The movie was severely lacking in variety.
stale	The movie had no novelty; it was just like movies they'd seen over and over before.
stodgy	The movie was unduly formal and traditional.
tedious	The movie was tiresome because it was so long, slow, or dull.
unexciting	The movie wasn't at all stimulating or thought-provoking.
wearisome	The movie was so lacking in interest that Michael and Beth were mentally tired out.

CURED!

*Golf without bunkers and hazards would be tame and **monotonous**. So would life.*

B. C. FORBES

bring

PART OF SPEECH	*verb*
DEFINITION	*to carry, convey, lead, or cause to go along to another place*

chaperone

accompany

escort

usher

transport

lead

schlepp

cures for the common word

accompany	**escort**	piggyback
attend	fetch	ride
back	gather	**schlepp**
bear	guide	shoulder
carry	heel	take
chaperone	hump	take along
companion	import	tote
conduct	**lead**	transfer
consort	lug	**transport**
convey	pack	truck
deliver	pick up	**usher**

CURED!

*You can **lead** a man to Congress, but you can't make him think.*

MILTON BERLE

Please **bring** the stars of the show backstage.

Choosing *bring* in this sentence is very neutral and doesn't tell us much about the speaker's perspective or opinion—about you or the stars of the show.

powerful remedies

Substitute an alternative remedy for *bring*:

Please _____ the stars of the show backstage.

accompany   You're being asked to come backstage along with the stars, suggesting you are a welcome participant as opposed to someone doing a job.

chaperone   As part of your task, you may need to ensure propriety or restrict the activity of the stars or others in some way.

escort   Choosing *escort* can give a sense of respect for the stars or can suggest that the stars require some supervision.

lead   In this case, you will go before the stars in order to show the way.

schlepp   *Schlepp* gives the sense that the person speaking isn't very impressed or thrilled about accompanying the stars backstage.

transport   This implies you'll need to use some sort of car, cart, etc., to convey the stars, since it's doubtful you'll need to physically carry them.

usher   You will lead the stars backstage and possibly introduce them to the appropriate person or people.

CURED!

*When you **escort** someone, escort him all the way to his destination; if you help someone, help him thoroughly.*

CHINESE PROVERB

certain

PART OF SPEECH   *adjective*
DEFINITION   *confident; free from doubt or reservation*

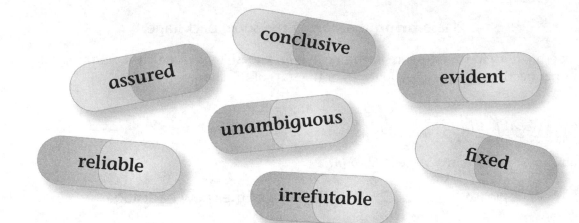

conclusive

assured

evident

unambiguous

reliable

fixed

irrefutable

cures for the common word

absolute	incontrovertible	secure
assured	indubitable	set
believing	infallible	sound
calm	**irrefutable**	sure
clear	known	true
conclusive	plain	**unambiguous**
convinced	positive	undeniable
definite	predestined	unequivocal
evident	real	unerring
firm	**reliable**	unmistakable
fixed	safe	unquestionable
guaranteed	sanguine	verifiable

CURED!

*We have no **reliable** guarantee that the afterlife will be any less exasperating than this one, have we?*

NOEL COWARD

The outcome of the election was **certain**.

In this sentence, we can't clearly tell whether the certainty of the election was perceived in a positive or negative light.

Substitute an alternative remedy for *certain*:

The outcome of the election was _____.

assured   The sense is that the outcome was promised or guaranteed in advance, and this can have either a positive or a negative connotation.

conclusive   The outcome served to settle a question.

evident   The outcome of the election is obvious and easily seen or understood.

fixed   This offers a negative connotation, implying that the outcome was arranged in advance privately and possibly dishonestly.

irrefutable   It would be impossible to deny or disprove the outcome.

reliable   People will be confident that the outcome is dependable, accurate, and honest.

unambiguous   The outcome has a single clearly defined meaning.

*If you think of paying court to the men in power, your eternal ruin is **assured**.*
STENDHAL [MARIE-HENRI BEYLE]

change

PART OF SPEECH	*verb*
DEFINITION	*to make different from what it is or from what it would be if left alone*

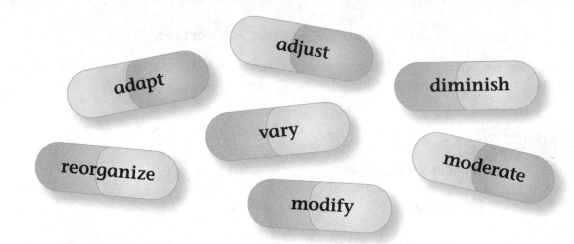

cures for the common word

accommodate	**modify**	revolutionize
adapt	modulate	shape
adjust	mutate	shift
alter	naturalize	substitute
alternate	recondition	tamper with
commute	redo	transfigure
convert	reform	transform
diminish	regenerate	translate
diverge	remake	transmute
diversify	remodel	transpose
evolve	renovate	turn
fluctuate	**reorganize**	vacillate
make over	replace	**vary**
make innovations	resolve	veer
moderate	restyle	warp

*Age does not **diminish** the extreme disappointment of having a scoop of ice cream fall from the cone.*

JIM FIEBIG

Martha always wants to **change** the rules in the middle of the game.

We can infer from this sentence that the speaker is not happy about the rule changing, but how unhappy may be better clarified by how and how much Martha wants to change the rules.

powerful remedies

Substitute an alternative remedy for *change*:

Martha always wants to _____ the rules in the middle of the game.

adapt   Martha wants to make logical or fitting changes that make sense.

adjust   Now Martha wants to change the rules so they fit or conform—but to her perspective and not necessarily to anyone else's.

diminish   Martha wants to put less emphasis on the rules of the game, perhaps because it's not going well for her.

moderate   Martha feels there are too many rules or they are too strict, so she wants to reduce the excessiveness of them.

modify   Martha wants to change the form or quality of the rules, but only slightly.

reorganize   Martha wants to completely rearrange the rules.

vary   Martha wants to change the rules slightly to avoid monotony.

*Not being able to control events, I control myself, and I **adapt** myself to them, if they do not adapt themselves to me.*

MICHEL DE MONTAIGNE

choose

PART OF SPEECH	*verb*
DEFINITION	*to select from a number of possible alternatives; to decide on and pick out*

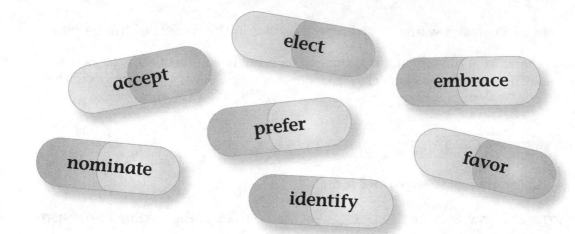

cures for the common word

accept	fancy	set aside
adopt	**favor**	settle upon
appoint	finger	sift out
cast	fix on	single out
co-opt	glean	slot
crave	**identify**	sort
cull	judge	tag
decide on	love	take
designate	name	tap
desire	**nominate**	want
determine	opt for	weigh
elect	predestined	will
embrace	**prefer**	winnow
excerpt	see fit	wish
extract	select	wish for

CURED!

*History will never **accept** difficulties as an excuse.*

JOHN F. KENNEDY

> This year the foundation will **choose** two charities to support.

Using *choose* in this sentence gives complete information but doesn't give us the sense of how the members of the foundation feel or think about the two charities.

powerful remedies

Substitute an alternative remedy for *choose*:

> This year the foundation will _____ two charities to support.

accept	The charities were suggested or offered (as opposed to sought out), and the foundation will respond affirmatively to supporting them.
elect	In this case, the charities were voted on and won the votes.
embrace	The foundation willingly and eagerly wants to support these two charities.
favor	The foundation prefers these two charities and may have treated them with partiality in comparison to other charities.
identify	This tells us that the foundation recognized these two charities; the connotation is that the foundation recognized *and* chose them.
nominate	The foundation is proposing these two charities to support.
prefer	The foundation members like these two charities better and value them more highly than others.

CURED!

*People say that life is the thing, but I **prefer** reading.*

LOGAN PEARSALL SMITH

common

PART OF SPEECH	adjective
DEFINITION	*ordinary; widespread; general; of frequent occurrence; usual; familiar*

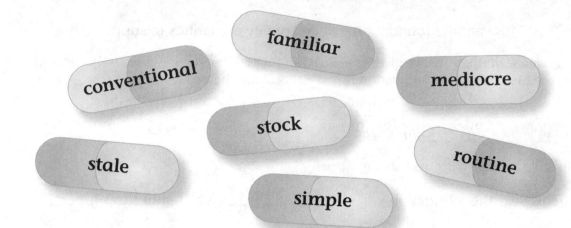

cures for the common word

accepted	habitual	**routine**
average	hackneyed	run-of-the-mill
banal	homely	**simple**
bourgeois	humdrum	**stale**
casual	informal	standard
characteristic	**mediocre**	stereotypical
colloquial	monotonous	**stock**
conventional	natural	trite
current	obscure	typical
customary	passable	undistinguished
daily	plain	universal
everyday	prevailing	unvaried
familiar	prevalent	usual
frequent	prosaic	wearisome
general	regular	workaday

*Great spirits have always faced violent protest from **mediocre** minds.*

ALBERT EINSTEIN

DIAGNOSIS *vague*

Claire selected a **common** theme for her term paper.

As the multiple definitions of this word indicate, *common* can mean such a wide variety of things—some positive and some negative—so we are unclear as to what it means in this sentence.

powerful remedies

Substitute an alternative remedy for *common*:

Claire selected a _____ theme for her term paper.

conventional   The theme is ordinary rather than different or original, but this doesn't usually have a negative connotation.

familiar   The theme is one known by many people.

mediocre   The theme is of only ordinary or moderate quality; it is barely adequate.

routine   The theme is unimaginative and in this sentence has a negative connotation—likely indicating the professor has seen this theme over and over.

simple   The theme is easy to understand, and we're not sure in this case if that's good or bad.

stale   The theme lacks originality or spontaneity or presents a perspective that many have presented before.

stock   Since *stock* means something kept regularly on hand, this theme might have been taken from a list online or some overused resource.

CURED!

*My religion is very **simple**. My religion is kindness.*

THE DALAI LAMA

correct

PART OF SPEECH   *adjective*
DEFINITION   *free from error; especially conforming to fact or truth*

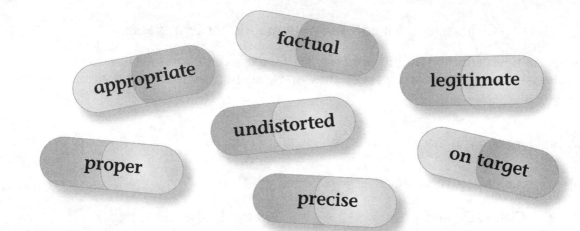

cures for the common word

actual	impeccable	right
amen	just	righteous
appropriate	**legitimate**	rigorous
equitable	nice	stone
exact	OK	strict
factual	**on target**	true
faithful	perfect	**undistorted**
faultless	**precise**	unmistaken
flawless	**proper**	veracious
for sure	regular	veridical

*Cyberspace: a consensual hallucination experienced daily by billions of **legitimate** operators, in every nation.*

WILLIAM GIBSON

DIAGNOSIS   *confusing*

Be sure to use the **correct** details in the brochure.

Especially in business, *correct* can mean much more than just the facts—it can refer to etiquette or tone—so we need more description of what *correct* means for the brochure.

powerful remedies

Substitute an alternative remedy for *correct*:

Be sure to use the _____ details in the brochure.

appropriate   The details should be suitable or fitting for this particular brochure.

factual   Be sure all details pertain to accurate facts.

legitimate   The details need to be in accordance with established or accepted patterns and standards.

on target   This is a slang way to say that the details should reach a particular audience or substantiate a point.

precise   The details should be exactly what you want to say, neither more nor less.

proper   The details should strictly belong or be applicable to the brochure, company, and/or image.

undistorted   The details should not be altered or misrepresented.

*In suggesting gifts: money is **appropriate**, and one size fits all.*
WILLIAM RANDOLPH HEARST

correct

PART OF SPEECH	*verb*
DEFINITION	*to set or make true, accurate, or right; to remove the errors or faults from*

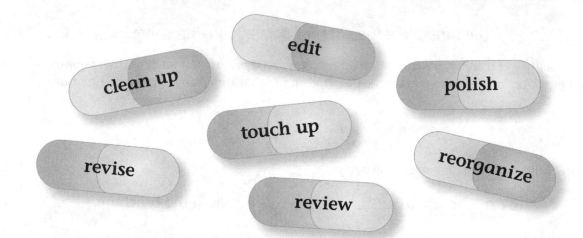

clean up · *edit* · *polish* · *touch up* · *revise* · *reorganize* · *review*

cures for the common word

alter
ameliorate
amend
better
change
clean up
cure
debug
do over
doctor
edit
emend
fiddle with
fix up
go over

help
improve
launder
make over
make right
mend
pay dues
pick up
polish
reclaim
reconstruct
rectify
redress
reform
regulate

remedy
remodel
reorganize
repair
retouch
review
revise
right
set right
set straight
shape up
straighten out
touch up
turn around
upgrade

CURED!

*He who does not get fun and enjoyment out of every day . . . needs to **reorganize** his life.*

GEORGE M. ADAMS

DIAGNOSIS *vague*

Lois will **correct** the article before it's published.

We know Lois will fix the article in some way, but using a more precise word will help us understand to what level or degree.

powerful remedies

Substitute an alternative remedy for *correct*:

Lois will _____ the article before it's published.

clean up   Lois will correct errors as well as look to rid the article of small details or wording that is considered undesirable.

edit   Now an accepted term to mean to revise or correct, *edit* may also imply a professional editor's review of the article.

polish   In addition to correcting errors, Lois will aim to refine and add elegance to the article.

reorganize   The article needs to undergo changes in organization.

review   Lois will examine the article with an eye to criticism or correction.

revise   Lois will fix or improve the article, or simply only update the information.

touch up   There may not even be errors in the article, but it could benefit from slight changes.

CURED!

*I **edit** out the bad stuff and deliver the good stuff. Seventy-five percent of all wine is awful.*

PETER MORRELL

decent

PART OF SPEECH   *adjective*
DEFINITION   *respectable; suitable; conforming to a recognized standard of good taste*

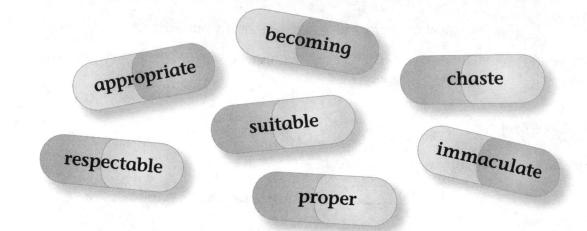

cures for the common word

adequate	fit	reserved
appropriate	fitting	**respectable**
approved	good	right
becoming	honest	spotless
befitting	honorable	stainless
chaste	**immaculate**	standard
clean	mannerly	straight
comely	modest	**suitable**
conforming	moral	trustworthy
continent	nice	unblemished
correct	noble	undefiled
decorous	presentable	untarnished
delicate	**proper**	upright
ethical	prudent	virtuous
fair	pure	worthy

CURED!

The great artists of the world are never Puritans, and seldom even ordinarily ***respectable****.*

HENRY LOUIS MENCKEN

DIAGNOSIS *vague*

Pat needs a **decent** dress for the party.

In this sentence, it's unclear if Pat's dress needs to be in good shape, in morally good taste, or something completely different.

powerful remedies

Substitute an alternative remedy for *decent*:

Pat needs a(n) _____ dress for the party.

appropriate — Pat's dress needs to be suitable and just right for this particular type of party.

becoming — Pat wants a dress that will have a pleasing effect and give her an attractive appearance.

chaste — Pat feels her dress should be conservative in style and not excessively ornamented.

immaculate — Pat needs her dress to be spotlessly clean, with every aspect of it in perfect condition.

proper — Pat's dress needs to conform to established standards for the occasion.

respectable — Pat hopes her dress will make a certain, esteemed impression on the attendees.

suitable — Pat would like her dress to be appropriate for the occasion and also fitting for her character.

*I present myself to you in a form **suitable** to the relationship I wish to achieve with you.*

LUIGI PIRANDELLO

develop

PART OF SPEECH *verb*
DEFINITION *to bring out the capabilities or possibilities of; to cause to grow or expand*

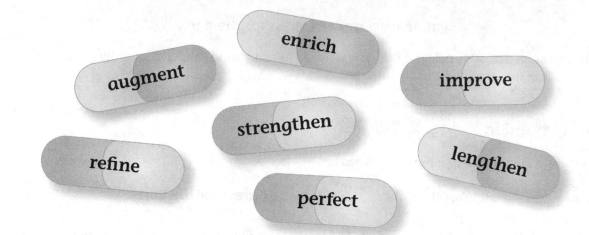

cures for the common word

actualize	enlarge	materialize
advance	**enrich**	**perfect**
amplify	evolve	polish
augment	exploit	promote
beautify	extend	realize
broaden	finish	**refine**
build up	heighten	**strengthen**
cultivate	**improve**	stretch
deepen	intensify	unfold
dilate	**lengthen**	widen
elaborate	magnify	work out

*How wonderful it is that nobody need wait a single moment before starting to **improve** the world.*

ANNE FRANK

The loan committee asked us to **develop** our business plan.

In order to provide the committee with exactly what they want, we need to know exactly what they want, and *develop* doesn't give us enough information.

powerful remedies

Substitute an alternative remedy for *develop*:

The loan committee asked us to _____ our business plan.

augment	The committee likes what we have but wants us to give more detail to the information we already have included.
enrich	We need to add or change information to make our plan more desirable.
improve	We need to raise the quality of the information in the business plan.
lengthen	The committee feels our plan is too slight and wants a more substantial document.
perfect	Our plan is pretty good, but the committee wants us to make it flawless—or as close as possible—to give us the best opportunity of approval.
refine	Our plan needs to be more precise or in clearer form.
strengthen	To increase our chances for a loan, the bank wants us to make our plan stronger—for example, by giving more information on our financial status.

CURED!

One thousand days to learn; ten thousand days to refine.

JAPANESE PROVERB

difficult

PART OF SPEECH	*adjective*
DEFINITION	*not easily or readily done*

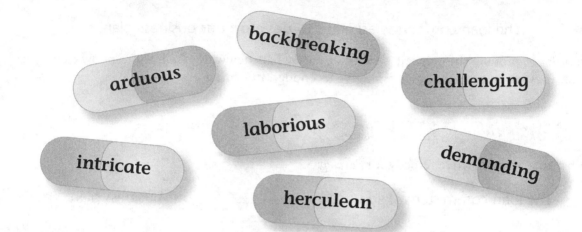

cures for the common word

ambitious	hard	prohibitive
arduous	hard-won	rigid
backbreaking	heavy	severe
bothersome	**herculean**	strenuous
burdensome	immense	titanic
challenging	**intricate**	toilsome
crucial	irritating	tough
demanding	labored	troublesome
effortful	**laborious**	trying
exacting	onerous	unyielding
formidable	painful	uphill
galling	problem	upstream
gargantuan	problematic	wearisome

CURED!

*To build may have to be the slow and **laborious** task of years.*
To destroy can be the thoughtless act of a single day.

SIR WINSTON CHURCHILL

A **difficult** job can wear you out, or it can be satisfying.

From this use of *difficult*, it's unclear whether we are talking about a job that is hard physically or mentally and in what way it is not easy.

powerful remedies

Substitute an alternative remedy for *difficult*:

A(n) _____ job can wear you out, or it can be satisfying.

arduous	The job is physically strenuous, requiring a great deal of energy and vigor.
backbreaking	The job is an exhausting physical task, demanding great effort and endurance.
challenging	Though the job is not easy, it's an undertaking that is stimulating.
demanding	The job requires more effort and time than is generally considered to be due.
herculean	The job is very hard to perform, requiring great physical or mental strength.
intricate	The job is complicated and hard to understand.
laborious	The job requires a lot of work, exertion, or perseverance either physically or mentally.

*The story of civilization is, in a sense, the story of engineering—that long and **arduous** struggle to make the forces of nature work for man's good.*

L. SPRAGUE DE CAMP

difficult

PART OF SPEECH	*adjective*
DEFINITION	*complicated; hard to comprehend*

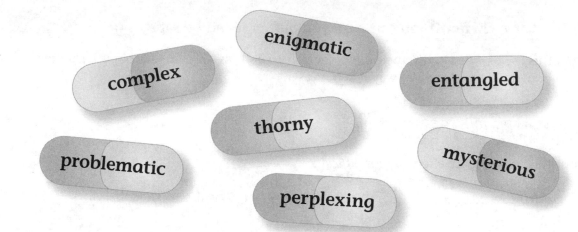

cures for the common word

abstract	formidable	paradoxical
abstruse	hard	**perplexing**
baffling	hidden	**problematic**
bewildering	inexplicable	profound
complex	intricate	puzzling
confounding	involved	rambling
confusing	knotty	subtle
dark	labyrinthine	tangled
deep	loose	**thorny**
delicate	meandering	ticklish
enigmatic	**mysterious**	troublesome
enigmatical	mystifying	unclear
entangled	obscure	unfathomable
esoteric	obstinate	unintelligible

CURED!

*Some problems are so **complex** that you have to be highly intelligent and well informed just to be undecided about them.*

LAURENCE JOHNSTON PETER

Romantic relationships can be **difficult**.

Difficult in this case is a little ambiguous. It has a negative connotation, but it doesn't give us the full picture of how the relationship is challenging.

powerful remedies

Substitute an alternative remedy for *difficult*:

Romantic relationships can be _____.

complex	Some relationships can be so complicated or intricate that they're hard to understand or deal with.
enigmatic	Relationships can be baffling, puzzling, and mysterious, which may be a positive to some people.
entangled	Relationships can be intertwined with difficulties, including anything from emotional to logistical complications.
mysterious	Relationships can involve secrets or unexplained aspects, which may have a positive or negative connotation.
perplexing	Relationships can be confusing and marked with uncertainty or doubt.
problematic	Relationships can make great mental demands that seem hard to comprehend, solve, or even believe.
thorny	Relationships can be full of difficulties or complexities; *thorny* clearly has a much more negative connotation.

CURED!

*The way of the troublemaker is **thorny**.*

AMERICAN UMPQUA INDIAN PROVERB

PART OF SPEECH	*adjective*
DEFINITION	*honest; straightforward; frank; candid*

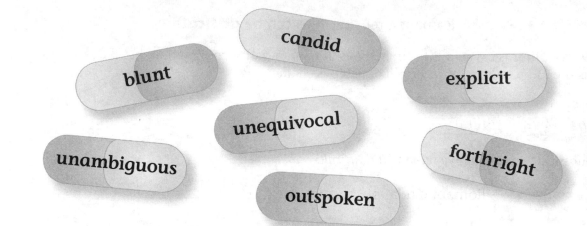

cures for the common word

absolute	frank	sincere
bald	genuine	straight
blunt	guileless	straightforward
candid	matter-of-fact	truthful
categorical	open	**unambiguous**
downright	**outspoken**	unconcealed
explicit	plain	undisguised
express	plain-spoken	**unequivocal**
forthright	point-blank	unreserved

CURED!

He was always smoothing and polishing himself, and in the end he became **blunt** *before he was sharp.*

G. C. (GEORG CHRISTOPH) LICHTENBERG

Betty was very **direct** in all her remarks.

Being *direct* can be considered admirable or impolite, so using a more precise alternative will let us know how we feel about Betty's remarks.

powerful remedies

Substitute an alternative remedy for *direct*:

Betty was very _____ in all her remarks.

blunt Betty spoke abruptly, which is not usually considered a positive way to speak.

candid Betty seemed to speak free from reservation or disguise, meaning she was being honest; candid often has the connotation of the honesty being refreshing.

explicit Betty fully and clearly expressed her remarks, leaving nothing she thought as merely implied.

forthright Betty's remarks were characterized by her direct manner or speech, without subtlety or evasion.

outspoken Betty was free and unreserved in her remarks; *outspoken* often has a negative connotation.

unambiguous There was no doubt about what Betty's remarks meant, because they expressed a single, clearly defined meaning.

unequivocal Betty's remarks were not subject to conditions or exceptions, leaving no doubt about her meaning.

*George Orwell's contention was that it is a sure sign of trouble when things can no longer be called by their right names and described in plain, **forthright** speech.*

CHRISTOPHER LASCH

do

PART OF SPEECH	*verb*
DEFINITION	*to perform, execute, carry out*

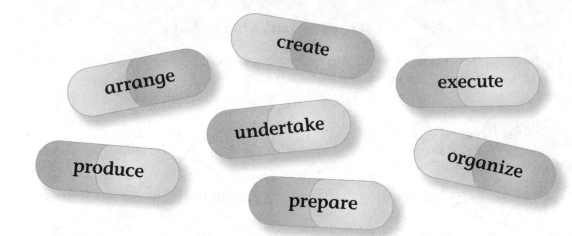

cures for the common word

accomplish	end	perform
achieve	engage in	perk
act	**execute**	**prepare**
arrange	finish	**produce**
bring about	fix	pull off
cause	fulfill	see to
complete	get ready	succeed
conclude	look after	take on
cook	make	transact
create	make ready	**undertake**
determine	move	wind up
discharge	operate	work
effect	**organize**	wrap up

*Don't agonize, **organize**.*

FLORYNCE KENNEDY

If you want to have a successful event, John at On Board Entertainment can **do** it.

We know that John is the right person to go to, but since the verb *do* can stand in for hundreds of actions, we don't have enough information about John's specific role in the successful event.

powerful remedies

Substitute an alternative remedy for *do*:

If you want to have a successful event, John at On Board Entertainment can _____ it.

arrange	*Arrange* can mean that John will plan the overall aspects or the details of the event.
create	The event will evolve from John's own thought and imagination.
execute	John will ensure that the event is carried out in accordance with an established plan—his, the client's, or both.
organize	John will coordinate each of the interdependent parts of the plan for united action—in this case, a successful event.
prepare	John may actually get ready each aspect of the event—from the smallest detail to the largest.
produce	John will supervise the entire event, contributing creatively and possibly also financially.
undertake	John has agreed to take it upon himself to work on this event and is committed to making it a success.

CURED!

*The significant problems we face cannot be solved at the same level of thinking we were at when we **created** them.*

ALBERT EINSTEIN

easy

PART OF SPEECH	*adjective*
DEFINITION	*capable of being accomplished or acquired with ease; posing no difficulty*

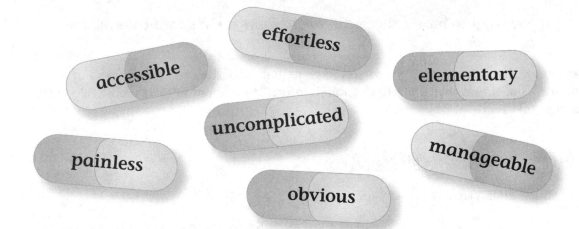

cures for the common word

accessible
apparent
basic
child's play
cinch
clear
comfortable
effortless
elementary
evident
facile
inconsiderable
light
little

manageable
manifest
mere
natural
no bother
no problem
no sweat
no trouble
obvious
painless
paltry
picnic
plain
plain sailing

pleasant
pushover
relaxed
royal
simple
slight
smooth
snap
straightforward
uncomplicated
undemanding
uninvolved
untroublesome
yielding

*The world is full of **obvious** things which nobody by any chance ever observes.*

SIR ARTHUR CONAN DOYLE

DIAGNOSIS *vague*

Professor Waddingham made the new math seem **easy**.

Thank goodness someone can make the new math seem easy, but in this sentence we're not sure exactly *how* the professor managed to make it less difficult.

powerful remedies

Substitute an alternative remedy for *easy*:

Professor Waddingham made the new math seem _____.

accessible	She showed us how to easily approach and use the math.
effortless	She taught us a way to learn the math that required little or no effort.
elementary	She helped us learn by showing us the fundamental and simplest aspects of the math.
manageable	She found a way to make us feel in control of learning the math instead of lost by it.
obvious	She was able to show us the math in a way that we easily understood.
painless	This is an informal way to say that she made learning the math seem like it required little or no hard work.
uncomplicated	She was able to make the math seem simple instead of complex or involved.

*Suffering, once accepted, loses its edge, for the terror of it lessens, and what remains is generally far more **manageable** than we had imagined.*

LESLEY HAZELTON

effective

PART OF SPEECH	*adjective*
DEFINITION	*producing the intended or expected result; adequate to accomplish a purpose*

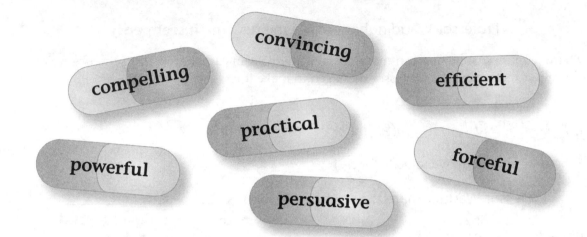

cures for the common word

able	energetic	resultant
active	**forceful**	serviceable
adequate	forcible	serving
capable	impressive	sound
cogent	live	striking
compelling	moving	successful
competent	operative	sufficient
convincing	**persuasive**	telling
direct	potent	trenchant
effectual	**powerful**	useful
efficacious	powerhouse	valid
efficient	**practical**	virtuous
emphatic	producing	yielding

CURED!

*It's pretty hard to be **efficient** without being obnoxious.*

KIN HUBBARD

The speechwriter used very **effective** language.

We can infer that the language was successful in getting the writer's point across well, or it evoked in the reader the writer's desired effect, but it's not clear how the language was used to accomplish the writer's goal.

powerful remedies

Substitute an alternative remedy for *effective*:

The speechwriter used very _____ language.

compelling   The language had a powerful and irresistible effect, engaging us to keep reading.

convincing   By the use of argument or evidence, the language brought us to a firm belief the writer intended for us.

efficient   The language functioned in the best possible manner with the least waste of time and effort; however, *efficient* doesn't lend itself toward a creative feel.

forceful   The writing was powerful and vigorous, as opposed to soft or gentle and coercing.

persuasive   The language was able to persuade us into thinking, seeing, or feeling just as the writer intended.

powerful   The writer used language with great reason, authority, or influence and impacted us—an ideal goal for a speech.

practical   The language used achieved the intended effect, but *practical* doesn't give the impression of a speech that was outstanding or that moved people to action.

CURED!

Being **powerful** *is like being a lady. If you have to tell people you are, you aren't.*

MARGARET THATCHER

emphasize

PART OF SPEECH	*verb*
DEFINITION	*to lay stress upon; to single out as important*

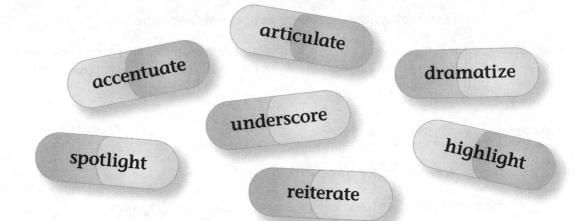

cures for the common word

accent
accentuate
affirm
articulate
assert
charge
dramatize
enlarge
enunciate
headline
highlight

impress
indicate
insist on
italicize
maintain
make clear
mark
pinpoint
play up
point out
press

prioritize
pronounce
punctuate
reiterate
repeat
rub in
spot
spotlight
underline
underscore
weight

CURED!

*A talent for drama is not a talent for writing, but is an ability to **articulate** human relationships.*

GORE VIDAL

Emphasize your work experience when applying for a job.

You always want to present yourself at your best when applying for a job, but in this sentence we don't have enough information about *how* exactly to best present your work experience.

powerful remedies

Substitute an alternative remedy for *emphasize*:

_____ your work experience when applying for a job.

accentuate	In addition to your other qualities, single out your work experience to present as important.
articulate	Formulate what you want to say about your work experience, and express your thoughts with clarity and effectiveness.
dramatize	Represent your work experience vividly, emotionally, or strikingly.
highlight	You want to present all of your positive attributes, but you want your work experience to be the most interesting or memorable part of your application.
reiterate	You want to mention your work experience repeatedly for emphasis.
spotlight	You have so many qualifications for the job, your work experience may be overshadowed, and you want to call particular attention to your experience.
underscore	Especially if you think your work experience is the key to winning the job—or you might not fully have other qualities the company is looking for—give extra weight to your experience.

CURED!

*Hard work **spotlights** the character of people: some turn up their sleeves, some turn up their noses, and some don't turn up at all.*

SAM EWIG

end

PART OF SPEECH	*verb*
DEFINITION	*to come to a conclusion; to terminate or cease*

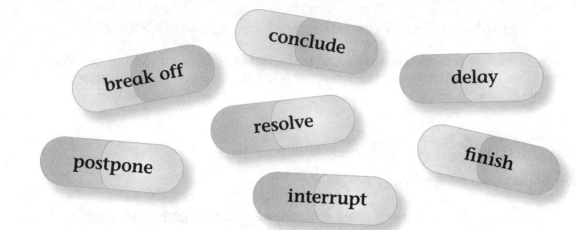

cures for the common word

abolish	culminate	perorate
abort	cut short	**postpone**
accomplish	**delay**	quit
achieve	determine	relinquish
break off	discontinue	**resolve**
break up	dispose of	settle
call off	dissolve	sew up
cease	drop	shut down
close	expire	stop
close out	**finish**	terminate
complete	get done	ultimate
conclude	give up	wind up
consummate	halt	wrap
crown	**interrupt**	wrap up

*Never **interrupt** your enemy when he is making a mistake.*

NAPOLEON BONAPARTE

We need to **end** the negotiations today.

Unfortunately, choosing *end* here doesn't give us any inclination as to whether the negotiations will end positively or negatively and successfully or not.

powerful remedies

Substitute an alternative remedy for *end*:

We need to _____ the negotiations today.

break off
Meaning to "stop suddenly," *break off* gives the impression that it was not a positive end of the day for either side in the negotiations.

conclude
The impression is not only that the negotiations will finish but also that the two sides will finally come to a decision or settlement.

delay
The negotiations will be put off to a later time, which may be OK, but sometimes *delay* can imply someone is hindering the progress.

finish
This is a neutral term—neither positive or negative—to say the two sides need to complete the negotiations.

interrupt
The negotiations will cease before they are complete, and the interruption may be for a reason that is not the fault of either side.

postpone
This indicates delaying the negotiations to another time, but it can also imply that they are delayed because one or both sides find the negotiations less important than originally thought.

resolve
This implies that the negotiators will reach a conclusion after a deliberation—hopefully one that's beneficial and satisfactory to both sides.

CURED!

*You may **delay**, but time will not.*

BENJAMIN FRANKLIN

energy

PART OF SPEECH	*noun*
DEFINITION	*the capacity for vigorous activity; abundant available power*

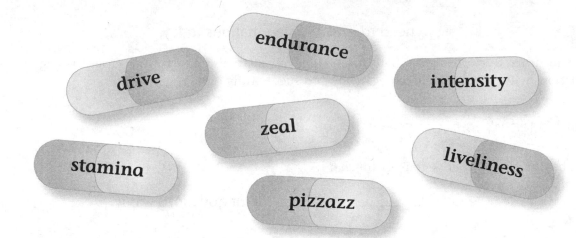

drive · endurance · intensity · zeal · liveliness · stamina · pizzazz

cures for the common word

animation	go	punch
ardor	initiative	spirit
birr	**intensity**	spontaneity
dash	juice	**stamina**
drive	life	steam
dynamism	**liveliness**	strength
élan	might	toughness
endurance	moxie	tuck
enterprise	muscle	vehemence
exertion	pep	verve
fire	**pizzazz**	vigor
force	pluck	vim
forcefulness	potency	vitality
fortitude	power	**zeal**
get-up-and-go	puissance	zest

CURED!

*Human kindness has never weakened the **stamina** or softened the fiber of a free people. A nation does not have to be cruel to be tough.*

FRANKLIN D. ROOSEVELT

Our yoga instructor Rada exhibits boundless **energy**.

The use of *energy* in this sentence doesn't firmly convey what impresses us about Rada—maybe her physical skills, her mental outlook, or her attitude.

powerful remedies

Substitute an alternative remedy for *energy*:

Our yoga instructor Rada exhibits boundless _____.

drive Rada is highly motivated and focused on a course toward her goals.

endurance Rada has the ability and strength to go on and on, despite fatigue.

intensity Rada has great energy, strength, and concentration during the yoga class—and likely outside of class also.

liveliness Rada is animated in her action and expression, which helps keep us all upbeat.

pizzazz Beyond lively, Rada has a downright dazzling style, flair, and energetic personality.

stamina Rada has a strength of physical constitution to endure fatigue and just about anything else.

zeal Rada has such an enthusiastic and tireless devotion to yoga as an ideal, which can be contagious.

CURED!

Endurance is patience concentrated.

THOMAS CARLYLE

enjoy

PART OF SPEECH	*verb*
DEFINITION	*to experience joy or satisfaction from; to take pleasure in*

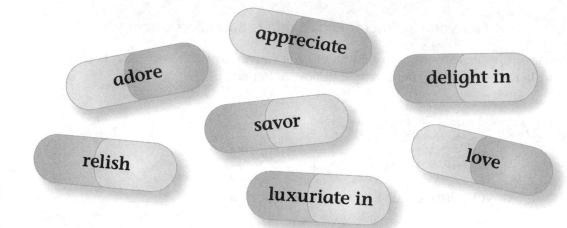

cures for the common word

adore	fancy	**luxuriate in**
appreciate	flip for	mind
be entertained	flip over	pleasure in
be pleased	funk	rejoice in
delight in	go	**relish**
dig	groove on	revel in
dote on	have fun	**savor**
drink in	like	savvy
eat up	**love**	take to

*The trouble with being punctual is that nobody's there to **appreciate** it.*

FRANKLIN P. JONES

I **enjoy** a break in my sunny backyard.

Choosing *enjoy* doesn't fully convey how much or why exactly I look forward to this break.

Substitute an alternative remedy for *enjoy*:

I _____ a break in my sunny backyard.

adore	Choosing *adore* comes closer to telling you how much I deeply love this escape.
appreciate	I'm grateful to have the time for and I truly value this break in the sunny yard.
delight in	Beyond simply liking my break in the yard, it gives me great joy.
love	Meaning "to like or desire enthusiastically," *love* is now a casual way to say how much I really, really enjoy my break in the sunny yard.
luxuriate in	This conjures up an image of lounging, reveling in my experience.
relish	This break is so wonderful that I eagerly look forward to it.
savor	I enjoy every minute of my break, knowing it's back to responsibilities when break time is over.

*A little nonsense now and then is **relished** by the wisest men.*

ROALD DAHL

enough

PART OF SPEECH	*adjective*
DEFINITION	*adequate for the want or need; sufficient for the purpose or to satisfy desire*

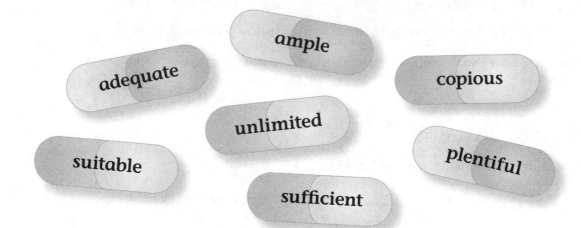

cures for the common word

abundant	complete	**plentiful**
acceptable	**copious**	replete
adequate	decent	satisfactory
ample	fed up	satisfying
bellyful	full	**sufficient**
bounteous	had it	sufficing
bountiful	last straw	**suitable**
comfortable	lavish	tolerable
competent	plenteous	**unlimited**

*To be witty is not enough. One must possess **sufficient** wit to avoid having too much of it.*

ANDRE MAUROIS

We have **enough** earthquake supplies for three people for a week.

In this sentence, *enough* for one person can be starvation (or excess) for others, so choosing a more precise word gives more information—or at least a better indication of how many supplies are stored.

powerful remedies

Substitute an alternative remedy for *enough*:

We have _____ earthquake supplies for three people for a week.

adequate	We're confident that we have supplies necessary for the basic requirements.
ample	We have more than enough supplies, which means we may be able to accommodate more people or for a longer duration.
copious	We have large quantities of supplies, more than ample, so we can invite in whoever needs help.
plentiful	We have a great quantity of supplies, but perhaps only if we stick to the prescribed number of people and/or duration anticipated.
sufficient	We have a quantity of supplies that can fulfill our need or requirement, but without being abundant.
suitable	Choosing *suitable* indicates that in addition to a proper amount of supplies, they are ones appropriate to the purpose.
unlimited	Not only do we have supplies immediately available, but we have a resource to provide an infinite amount for as many and as long as we need.

CURED!

*The supply of words in the world market is **plentiful** but the demand is falling. Let deeds follow words now.*

LECH WALESA

excellent

PART OF SPEECH	*adjective*
DEFINITION	*of the highest or finest quality; exceptionally good of its kind*

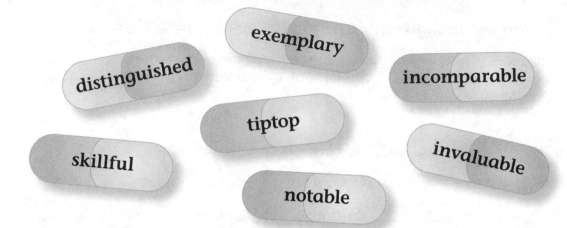

distinguished

exemplary

incomparable

tiptop

skillful

invaluable

notable

cures for the common word

accomplished	first-rate	remarkable
admirable	good	select
attractive	great	**skillful**
champion	high	splendid
choice	**incomparable**	sterling
desirable	**invaluable**	striking
distinctive	magnificent	superb
distinguished	meritorious	superior
estimable	**notable**	superlative
exceptional	noted	supreme
exemplary	outstanding	**tiptop**
exquisite	peerless	top-notch
fine	premium	transcendent
first	priceless	unsurpassed
first-class	prime	wonderful

CURED!

*In every phenomenon the beginning remains always the most **notable** moment.*

THOMAS CARLYLE

Katie has proved to be an **excellent** CEO.

When Katie took the position of CEO, we anticipated she would be excellent—an expectation she lived up to—but *excellent* doesn't give us a clear idea of the criteria on which we're basing our assessment.

powerful remedies

Substitute an alternative remedy for *excellent*:

Katie has proved to be a(n) _____ CEO.

distinguished   Katie stands above others in her character, achievements, and reputation.

exemplary   Katie is commendable and worthy of high praise and imitation.

incomparable   Katie's performance is beyond comparison—matchless and unequaled.

invaluable   Katie has done such a fine job that she has proved to be priceless, and the company would suffer greatly if she ever left.

notable   Katie is worthy of notice because of her outstanding work.

skillful   Katie has shown great knowledge, skill, and aptitude at her position as CEO.

tiptop   This is an informal way to say that Katie's work is of the highest quality.

CURED!

*Jackie Robinson, as an athlete and as someone who was trying to make a stand for equality, he was **exemplary**.*

KAREEM ABDUL-JABBAR

exciting

PART OF SPEECH	*adjective*
DEFINITION	*producing excitement or strong feeling in; stirring; thrilling; exhilarating*

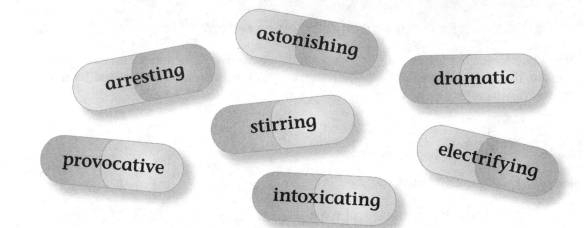

cures for the common word

animating	flashy	overwhelming
appealing	heady	**provocative**
arousing	hectic	racy
arresting	impelling	rip-roaring
astonishing	impressive	rousing
bracing	interesting	sensational
breathtaking	**intoxicating**	showy
dangerous	intriguing	spine-tingling
dramatic	lively	stimulating
electrifying	melodramatic	**stirring**
exhilarating	mind-blowing	thrilling
eye-popping	moving	titillating
far-out	neat	wild
fine	overpowering	zestful

*Perhaps of all the creations of man language is the most **astonishing**.*
LYTTON STRACHEY

President Kennedy was an **exciting** speaker.

Almost anyone who ever heard Kennedy speak—in person or on tape—likely felt strong emotion, but *exciting* doesn't specifically describe how you or I might have been affected by hearing him speak.

Substitute an alternative remedy for *exciting*:

President Kennedy was a(n) _____ speaker.

arresting
He had a way of attracting and holding—practically commanding—the attention of a crowd.

astonishing
He was a great and impressive speaker, to the surprise of his detractors.

dramatic
He spoke in a way that was sensational and thrilling.

electrifying
His speaking was sometimes shocking but definitely caused a surge of emotion.

intoxicating
Listening to him speak made people enthusiastic and exhilarated, almost light-headed.

provocative
He sometimes said things that were controversial, tending to stimulate—or provoke—discussion.

stirring
As well as rousing stimulating discussion, he could also rouse people to strong action.

CURED!

*Beauty is often worse than wine; **intoxicating** both the holder and beholder.*
JOHN ZIMMERMAN

fast

PART OF SPEECH	*adjective*
DEFINITION	*quick; swift; moving or able to move, operate, function, or take effect quickly*

brisk

agile

dashing

swift

nimble

expeditious

hasty

cures for the common word

accelerated
active
agile
breakneck
brisk
chop-chop
dashing
double time
electric
expeditious
expeditive
flashing
fleet

fleeting
flying
hair-trigger
hasty
hot
hurried
hypersonic
instant
lickety-split
like crazy
mercurial
nimble
PDQ

posthaste
presto
pronto
quick
racing
rapid
ready
screamin'
snap
snappy
swift
velocious
winged

CURED!

"

*The race is not always to the **swift**, nor the battle to the strong but that's the way to bet.*

DAMON RUNYON

"

Everyone agreed that Boomer ran the dog course at a **fast** pace.

Choosing to use *fast* gives a pretty vivid image of Boomer racing the course, but there are a few instances where *fast* isn't the best way to run a course. The following alternatives tell us more.

Substitute an alternative remedy for *fast*:

> Everyone agreed that Boomer ran the dog course at a(n) _____ pace.

agile	Boomer was quick and well coordinated in his movements, and he also displayed an ability to think quickly, reacting well to course changes.
brisk	Boomer's movements were marked by speed and vigor.
dashing	As Boomer ran, he exhibited a spirited and lively energy as well as elegance.
expeditious	Boomer acted with speed and efficiency, though *expeditious* gives us no clue as to how gracefully he performed.
hasty	Boomer ran fast, but choosing *hasty* often carries a negative connotation, implying he was unduly quick and rash in his movements and choices.
nimble	Boomer was quick and light on his feet, moving with rapid ease.
swift	Not only was Boomer moving with great speed, acting and reacting quickly and cleverly, *swift* can also invoke a wonderful image of joy and freedom.

CURED!

*One cool judgment is worth a thousand **hasty** counsels. The thing to do is to supply light and not heat.*

WOODROW WILSON

feel

PART OF SPEECH	*verb*
DEFINITION	*to perceive or examine by touch*

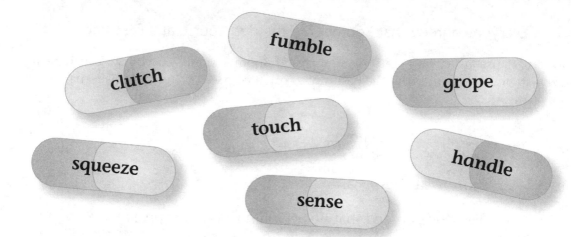

cures for the common word

caress	**grope**	press
clasp	**handle**	**sense**
clutch	manipulate	**squeeze**
explore	maul	stroke
finger	palm	test
fondle	palpate	thumb
frisk	paw	tickle
fumble	perceive	**touch**
grapple	pinch	try
grasp	ply	twiddle
grip	poke	wield

CURED!

*Gentlemen, it is better to have died as a small boy than to **fumble** this football.*

JOHN HEISMAN

Finally, Eric could **feel** the rescue rope.

Choosing *feel* here doesn't tell us anything about the circumstances of why Eric is feeling for the rope; whereas, the following alternatives give us a much more vivid image of the situation.

powerful remedies

Substitute an alternative remedy for *feel*:

Finally, Eric could _____ the rescue rope.

clutch	Eric is holding the rope tightly, or attempting to grasp it, indicating he may be about to fall if he doesn't seize it quickly.
fumble	Eric is feeling about clumsily for the rope; perhaps he just can't reach it.
grope	Eric is blindly feeling about with his hands with some uncertainty because he can't see the rope.
handle	Even if the rope might be difficult to grasp, Eric is able to manage it.
sense	Eric has so much experience climbing that he has an intuitive or acquired perception of where the rope is.
squeeze	Eric is able to press the rope gently, maybe just to be sure it's really there if needed.
touch	Eric can feel the rope, and this is more a matter of information than giving us any clue to his situation.

CURED!

*Love is blind. That is why he always proceeds by **touch**.*

FRENCH PROVERB

fill

PART OF SPEECH	*verb*
DEFINITION	*to occupy to the full capacity*

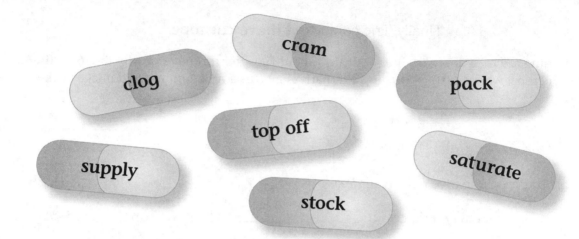

cram

clog

pack

top off

supply

saturate

stock

cures for the common word

block
brim over
bulge out
charge
choke
clog
close
congest
cram
crowd
distend
fulfill
furnish
glut
gorge

heap
impregnate
inflate
jam-pack
lade
load
meet
occupy
overflow
pack
permeate
pervade
plug
pump up
ram

replenish
sate
satiate
satisfy
saturate
shoal
stock
store
stretch
stuff
suffuse
supply
swell
take up
top off

CURED!

*The first forty years of life give us the text; the next thirty **supply** the commentary on it.*

ARTHUR SCHOPENHAUER

The local parks departments **fill** the streams with fish.

We know that fish are being added to the streams, but surprisingly, *fill* doesn't tell us to what degree, nor does it tells us if this is a good or bad thing.

powerful remedies

Substitute an alternative remedy for *fill*:

The local parks departments _____ the streams with fish.

clog	They put in so many fish that the streams are choked up, and it's hard to swim or boat in them.
cram	They have forced in more fish than the streams can easily hold, which is not healthy for the fish or the environment.
pack	The departments have crowded the fish together, perhaps in one set-off area of each stream.
saturate	This implies that the streams are completely packed, but *saturate* doesn't carry the same negative connotation as *cram*.
stock	The parks departments have added fish to the streams to have an appropriate number available.
supply	The departments have added fish to the streams, but the connotation here is that the streams were lacking the requisite amount.
top off	This is an informal term to indicate that the departments added just a few fish, because the streams were almost full to begin with.

*Next to a circus there ain't nothing that **packs** up and tears out faster than the Christmas spirit.*

KIN HUBBARD

PART OF SPEECH	*adjective*
DEFINITION	*conclusive or decisive; coming to the end; last in place, order, or time*

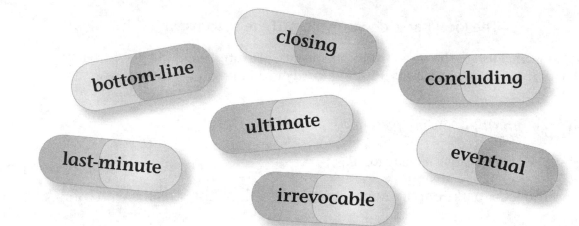

cures for the common word

absolute	determinative	latest
bottom-line	ending	latter
closing	**eventual**	settled
concluding	finished	supreme
crowning	finishing	swan song
decided	hindmost	terminal
decisive	incontrovertible	terminating
definite	irrefutable	**ultimate**
definitive	**irrevocable**	unanswerable
determinate	**last-minute**	unappealable

CURED!

*Final thoughts are so, you know, final. Let's call them **closing** words.*
CRAIG ARMSTRONG

DIAGNOSIS *vague*

The company's **final** decision regarding pay increases surprised us.

Though it's clear we were surprised by the decision, *final* doesn't indicate much about what was involved in the decision or how we feel about it.

powerful remedies

Substitute an alternative remedy for *final*:

The company's _____ decision regarding pay increases surprised us.

bottom-line	Whether we like the decision or not, it isn't going to change.
closing	There were negotiations or discussion on the topic, and the decision concludes those negotiations.
concluding	This implies that the decision was determined by reasoning, and the connotation is that we believe careful consideration was given to the decision.
eventual	Even though we were surprised, we knew a decision was expected at some point due to a process already begun and ongoing.
irrevocable	The company's decision is unalterable, so it cannot be changed or recalled.
last-minute	The company's decision was made just prior to a deadline.
ultimate	The company's decision was the final conclusion, ending a series of discussions.

CURED!

*It is easy to answer the **ultimate** questions—it saves you bothering with the immediate ones.*

JOHN OSBORNE

fine

PART OF SPEECH   *adjective*
DEFINITION   *of superior or best quality; excellent*

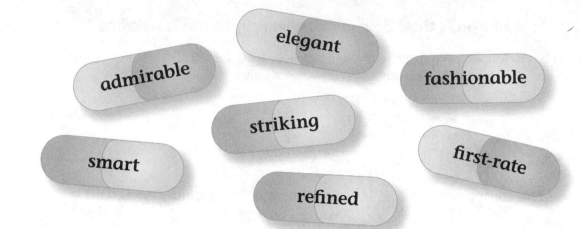

cures for the common word

accomplished	first-class	select
aces	**first-rate**	showy
admirable	five-star	skillful
attractive	good-looking	**smart**
beautiful	great	spiffy
capital	handsome	splendid
choice	lovely	**striking**
dandy	magnificent	subtle
elegant	ornate	superior
exceptional	outstanding	supreme
expensive	pleasant	top-notch
exquisite	rare	well-made
fashionable	**refined**	wicked

*I sometimes give myself **admirable** advice, but I am incapable of taking it.*
MARY WORTLEY MONTAGU

Dorothy's parents thought Ray was a **fine** choice as their daughter's date to the country club dinner.

In this sentence, we're unsure if Dorothy's parents found their daughter's date as merely adequate or an excellent surprise—we need more information.

powerful remedies

Substitute an alternative remedy for *fine*:

Dorothy's parents thought Ray was a(n) _____ choice as their daughter's date to the country club dinner.

admirable	Ray is a young man who inspires approval and respect—by his character or his actions.
elegant	Ray is gracefully refined and dignified.
fashionable	Ray has a stylish way of dressing.
first-rate	Ray is foremost in quality above other young men Dorothy (or her parents) might have considered as her date.
refined	Ray shows a well-bred character, manner, and feelings.
smart	Ray has a dashing, neat, and trim appearance.
striking	Ray has an impressively attractive appearance.

*One of the most **striking** differences between a cat and a lie is that the cat has only nine lives.*

MARK TWAIN

finish

PART OF SPEECH	*verb*
DEFINITION	*to get done*

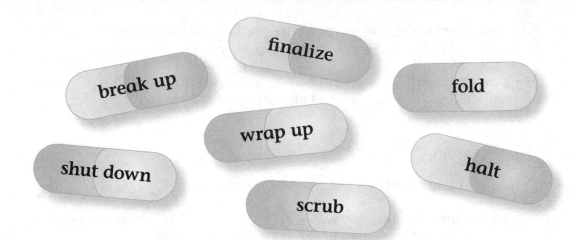

finalize

break up

fold

wrap up

shut down

halt

scrub

cures for the common word

accomplish	crown	mop up
achieve	culminate	perfect
bag it	deplete	round off
break up	determine	scratch
carry through	discharge	**scrub**
cease	end	settle
chuck	execute	sew up
clinch	exhaust	**shut down**
close	**finalize**	shutter
complete	**fold**	stop
conclude	fulfill	terminate
consume	**halt**	wrap
cool it	make	**wrap up**

CURED!

*The United Nations is presently unable to **break up** a skirmish between two warring Girl Scout factions, so how they're supposed to aid the world is an even bigger conundrum.*

ARTHUR LOTTI

DIAGNOSIS   *vague*

> Karen and her crew had to **finish** filming at midnight.

Though we know filming had to cease, *finish* doesn't tell us whether the filming was completed or only interrupted.

powerful remedies

Substitute an alternative remedy for *finish*:

> Karen and her crew had to ＿＿＿＿＿＿＿ filming at midnight.

break up   The filming was disrupted for some reason—and not in a good way.

finalize   They were in the process of putting the entire filming of a movie in final form.

fold   This is an informal way to say that they were forced to close down filming.

halt   They had to stop filming for the evening, though we don't know if it's temporarily or permanently.

scrub   This is a slang way to say the filming has been done away with—just plain canceled.

shut down   This is a more traditional way of saying the filming was ended but not completed.

wrap up   This is the movie and TV term for completing the filming of the final scene.

*We are not so much concerned if you are slow as when you come to a **halt**.*
CHINESE PROVERB

funny

PART OF SPEECH *adjective*
DEFINITION *humorous; causing amusement or laughter; comical*

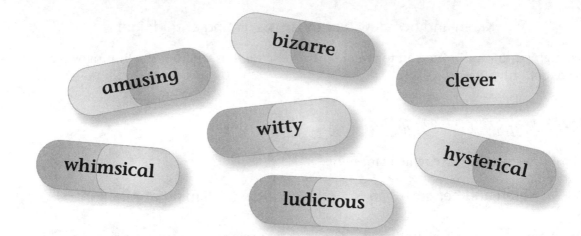

cures for the common word

absurd	gay	playful
amusing	good-humored	priceless
antic	hilarious	rich
a scream	humorous	ridiculous
bizarre	**hysterical**	riotous
blithe	jocular	risible
capricious	joking	side-splitting
clever	jolly	silly
comical	killing	slapstick
diverting	knee-slapping	sportive
droll	laughable	uncommon
entertaining	**ludicrous**	unusual
facetious	merry	**whimsical**
farcical	mirthful	**witty**

CURED!

*The desire to seem **clever** often keeps us from being so.*
FRANÇOIS VI DUKE (DUC) DE LA ROCHEFOUCAULD

Michael told us a **funny** story.

In this sentence, *funny* doesn't tell us what exactly was funny about Michael's story—whether it made us laugh, was unusual, or something different.

powerful remedies

Substitute an alternative remedy for *funny*:

Michael told us a(n) _____ story.

amusing	The story was entertaining or diverting, so it raised a smile but wasn't uproarious.
bizarre	The story was strikingly unconventional and far-fetched, and it led us to wonder if it was true or not.
clever	The details or plot of the story were original, and the connotation is that the story was intriguing.
hysterical	The story was so extremely funny we were laughing uncontrollably.
ludicrous	The story was laughable because of some obvious absurdity or incongruity.
whimsical	The story was lighthearted and given to whimsy or fancy.
witty	The story was quick and clever in its amusing insights.

CURED!

> *A **witty** saying proves nothing.*
>
> FRANÇOIS-MARIE AROUET VOLTAIRE

get

PART OF SPEECH *verb*
DEFINITION *to come into possession or use of; to acquire as a result of action or effort*

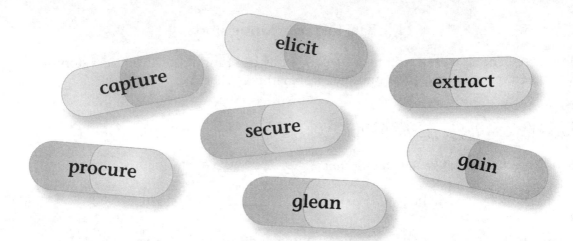

cures for the common word

access	educe	parlay
accomplish	**elicit**	pick up
achieve	evoke	**procure**
acquire	extort	pull
annex	**extract**	rack up
attain	fetch	realize
bag	**gain**	reap
build up	**glean**	receive
buy out	grab	score
capture	inherit	**secure**
clean up	land	snag
come by	lock up	snap up
cop	make	take
draw	net	wangle
earn	obtain	win

CURED!

*The good we **secure** for ourselves is precarious and uncertain—until it is secured for all of us and incorporated into our common life.*

JANE ADDAMS

I'd like to **get** more information from the president before I accept his proposal.

We're unsure of the nature of the proposal as well as how to go about getting more information from the president.

powerful remedies

Substitute an alternative remedy for *get*:

I'd like to _____ more information from the president before I accept his proposal.

capture	In a different context, this might mean obtaining the information by force or skill, but now it can also imply that I'm going to gather or record the information from different sources.
elicit	I'm going to draw the information from somewhere or someone, which still has a negative connotation.
extract	Though this might indicate drawing out by force, it can also mean to deduce or interpret information based on several factors.
gain	I'm going to acquire the information by my devoted research.
glean	I'm discovering information, a little at a time, from being alert to different resources I've investigated or things people have said.
procure	I'm going to obtain the information by some special means; the connotation is that it may be by unscrupulous and indirect means.
secure	I'm going to get possession of information from a dependable source.

*Who has confidence in himself will **gain** the confidence of others.*

LEIB LAZAROW

give

PART OF SPEECH	*verb*
DEFINITION	*to impart or communicate*

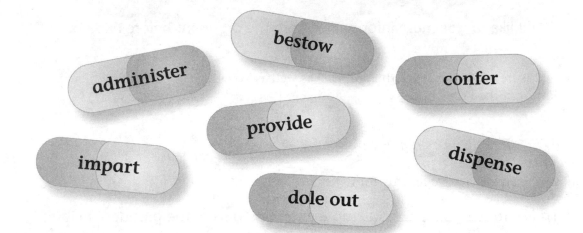

administer
bestow
confer
provide
impart
dispense
dole out

cures for the common word

accord	distribute	permit
administer	**dole out**	pony up
ante up	donate	present
award	endow	**provide**
bequeath	entrust	relinquish
bestow	fork over	remit
cede	furnish	sell
commit	grant	shell out
confer	hand	subsidize
consign	**impart**	supply
convey	lease	throw in
deed	let have	transfer
deliver	parcel out	transmit
dish out	part with	vouchsafe
dispense	pass out	will

CURED!

*Sometimes I need what only you can **provide**—your absence.*

ASHLEIGH BRILLIANT

Give advice sparingly.

This is usually a good idea, but choosing *give* is very neutral, and doesn't tell us much about the intent behind the advice given and the reaction of the advisee.

Substitute an alternative remedy for *give*:

_____ advice sparingly.

administer   The advice is intended to contribute assistance, perhaps in a formal way.

bestow   The advice is being presented as a gift—or that is the intention of the giver, even if the receiver may not feel that way.

confer   The advice is being offered as a favor or honor, which may or may not be received with appreciation.

dispense   The advice is being distributed in parts or portions and has a connotation of being given without much emotion.

dole out   This is an informal way of saying the advice will be given in portions.

impart   Meaning "to tell, relate, and pass down," *impart* gives the sense of someone wise and knowledgeable sharing their wisdom—and it's gratefully received.

provide   The advice—almost like simple facts and information—is made available.

People who have given us their complete confidence believe that they have a right to ours. The inference is false; a gift **confers** *no rights.*

FRIEDRICH WILHELM NIETZSCHE

PART OF SPEECH	*verb*
DEFINITION	*to move or proceed, especially to or from something*

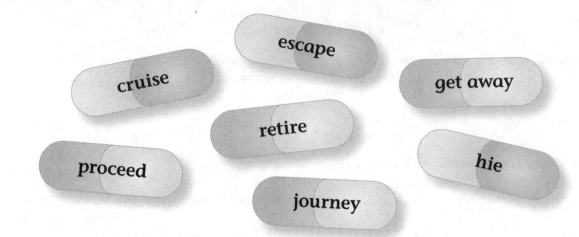

cures for the common word

abscond	get going	quit
advance	**hie**	repair
approach	hightail	**retire**
beat it	**journey**	run away
bug out	lam	shove off
cruise	leave	skip out
decamp	light out	split
depart	mosey	take flight
escape	move	take off
exit	pass	tool
fare	**proceed**	travel
flee	progress	vamoose
fly	pull out	wend
get away	push on	withdraw

CURED!

> *In what other business can a guy my age drink martinis, smoke cigars and sing? I think all people who **retire** ought to go into show business. I've been retired all my life.*
>
> GEORGE BURNS

DIAGNOSIS *vague*

In the morning, we'll **go** to the tropical island by boat.

Choosing *go* for this sentence doesn't give us much information about the speed or urgency of our journey or the motivations for it.

powerful remedies

Substitute an alternative remedy for *go*:

In the morning, we'll _____ to the tropical island by boat.

cruise	This gives us the feeling of a leisurely pleasure trip to the island.
escape	We are going to slip away to that tropical refuge, probably from the daily routine or problems we'd like a break from.
get away	We're going to take a vacation to the island.
hie	We're in a hurry to get to the sunny beaches on that island.
journey	Beyond heading for our destination, we're going to take our time as we go the long distance.
proceed	We're heading to the island, after an interruption of our trip.
retire	This implies we are going to the island for some privacy—or are now going to be enjoying a work-free life.

CURED!

*To travel is to take a **journey** into yourself.*

DENA KAYE

good

PART OF SPEECH *adjective*
DEFINITION *pleasant; enjoyable*

gratifying

commendable

honorable

wonderful

welcome

satisfying

valuable

cures for the common word

acceptable	first-class	serviceable
ace	functional	shipshape
admirable	**gratifying**	sound
agreeable	great	spanking
bully	**honorable**	splendid
capital	marvelous	sterling
choice	nice	stupendous
commendable	pleasing	super
competent	positive	superb
congenial	precious	superior
deluxe	prime	tip-top
excellent	reputable	**valuable**
exceptional	**satisfying**	**welcome**
favorable	select	**wonderful**

CURED!

*Say encouraging words to young people, make them feel **welcome** on the planet Earth (many do not). Show by example that we don't need all we have in order to be happy and productive.*

PAUL LUTUS

Volunteering gives most people a **good** feeling.

It's true that most people feel they receive more from volunteering than they give, but *good* doesn't adequately express how volunteering makes most people feel.

powerful remedies

Substitute an alternative remedy for *good*:

Volunteering gives most people a(n) _____ feeling.

commendable   Our volunteering is perceived by others as praiseworthy.

gratifying   Volunteering gives us a pleasing feeling of satisfaction.

honorable   We feel we are doing something creditable based on high principles and character.

satisfying   Our volunteering fulfills our expectations, giving a sense of full contentment.

valuable   We feel we're contributing in a helpful way, one we hope is worthy of respect.

welcome   Volunteering gives us an agreeable feeling of pleasure or satisfaction—a feeling maybe we don't often experience.

wonderful   Volunteering is beyond good, it's great, excellent, marvelous—so true.

CURED!

*Education is a **wonderful** thing. If you couldn't sign your name you'd have to pay cash.*

RITA MAE BROWN

good

PART OF SPEECH	*adjective*
DEFINITION	*having the qualities that are desirable or distinguishing in a particular thing; skille*

accomplished
experienced
masterful
trustworthy
talented
responsible
skillful

cures for the common word

able	**experienced**	serviceable
accomplished	expert	**skillful**
adept	first-rate	suitable
adroit	**masterful**	suited
au fait	proficient	**talented**
capable	proper	thorough
clever	qualified	trained
competent	reliable	**trustworthy**
dexterous	**responsible**	useful
efficient	satisfactory	wicked

CURED!

Responsible artists try to affect you sensually in a way that enlarges your experience.

PAULINE KAEL

Jack is a **good** canoe builder.

In this sentence, we understand that Jack is capable of building an outrigger, but it doesn't give us a clear idea of the extent of his training and skills.

Substitute an alternative remedy for *good*:

Jack is a(n) _____ canoe builder.

accomplished Jack is good at what he does as the result of his practice or training, and the implication is that his work is much above average.

experienced Jack's skill or wisdom comes through his experience.

masterful Jack's skills are beyond good, having and reflecting the power and skill of a master.

responsible Without indicating his skill level, Jack has shown that we can depend on him in terms of honesty in his work and his dealings with us.

skillful Jack is very good at his trade.

talented Beyond skilled, Jack is creative or artistic in his work.

trustworthy Jack's skills and performance are deserving of trust or confidence.

CURED!

*The only way to make a man **trustworthy** is to trust him.*

HENRY STIMSON

PART OF SPEECH	*adjective*
DEFINITION	*important; eminent; distinguished; remarkable or outstanding*

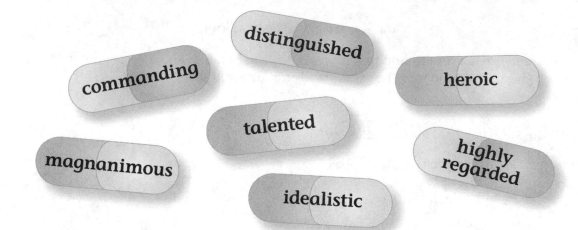

cures for the common word

august	**highly regarded**	paramount
capital	honorable	primary
celebrated	**idealistic**	principal
chief	illustrious	prominent
commanding	impressive	puissant
dignified	leading	regal
distinguished	lofty	remarkable
eminent	lordly	renowned
exalted	**magnanimous**	royal
excellent	major	stately
famous	noble	sublime
glorious	notable	superior
grand	noted	superlative
heroic	outstanding	**talented**

*The most **heroic** word in all languages is revolution.*

EUGENE DEBS

As a **great** leader, Nelson Mandela listens as well as he speaks.

In this sentence, *great* doesn't give us enough information to explain why Nelson Mandela is so highly thought of.

powerful remedies

Substitute an alternative remedy for *great*:

As a(n) _____ leader, Nelson Mandela listens as well as he speaks.

commanding	President Mandela has an imposing and authoritative presence.
distinguished	President Mandela is a wise man of great dignity, as well as an eminent and distinctive leader, as evidenced in part by his great accomplishments.
heroic	President Mandela has displayed the character and attributes of a hero, showing his boldness and daring under extreme measures.
highly regarded	President Mandela is held in high esteem and respect.
idealistic	President Mandela's beliefs are of high and noble principles, though *idealistic* can carry a connotation of unrealistic.
magnanimous	President Mandela is generous in his forgiving of insult and injury, free from petty resentfulness or vindictiveness.
talented	President Mandela exhibits special skills and abilities.

CURED!

"
*Nothing is more **idealistic** than a journalist on the defensive.*
MELVIN MADDOCKS
"

grow

PART OF SPEECH	*verb*
DEFINITION	*to expand or increase gradually by concerted effort*

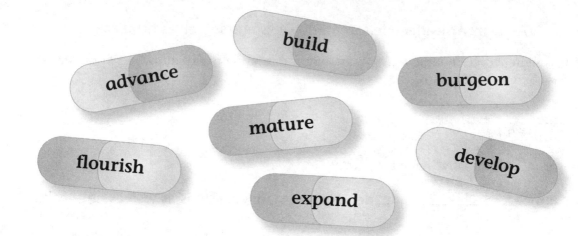

advance · build · burgeon · mature · flourish · develop · expand

cures for the common word

abound	fill out	pullulate
advance	**flourish**	raise
age	gain	ripen
amplify	germinate	rise
arise	heighten	shoot
augment	increase	spread
breed	issue	sprout
build	luxuriate	stem
burgeon	maturate	stretch
cultivate	**mature**	swell
develop	mount	thicken
dilate	multiply	thrive
enlarge	originate	turn
expand	produce	wax
extend	propagate	widen

CURED!

*I hate the man who **builds** his name on the ruins of another's fame.*

JOHN GAY

In going back to school, Christine knows both her knowledge and experience will **grow**.

We know that Christine's growth will be a positive experience, but *grow* doesn't clearly tell us what she is hoping for.

powerful remedies

Substitute an alternative remedy for *grow*:

In going back to school, Christine knows both her knowledge and experience will _____.

advance   Christine knows her education will move her forward in life.

build   Christine realizes her knowledge and experience will increase and strengthen.

burgeon   This implies Christine's knowledge and experience will develop quickly.

develop   Christine is hoping to build her skills to a more advanced level.

expand   Christine realizes she is extending both the volume and the scope of her knowledge.

flourish   Christine's hoping she'll thrive in a period of her highest productivity.

mature   Christine believes her knowledge and experience will evolve toward fuller development.

CURED!

*You can't say civilization don't **advance** . . . in every war they kill you in a new way.*

WILL ROGERS

happy

PART OF SPEECH   *adjective*
DEFINITION   *enjoying or showing joy or pleasure or good fortune*

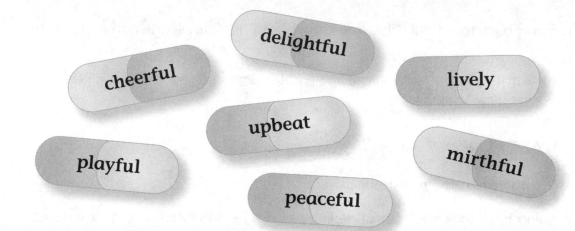

cheerful   delightful   lively   upbeat   playful   mirthful   peaceful

cures for the common word

blessed	gay	overjoyed
blissful	glad	**peaceful**
blithe	gleeful	peppy
captivated	gratified	perky
cheerful	hopped up	**playful**
chipper	intoxicated	pleasant
content	jolly	pleased
convivial	joyous	satisfied
delighted	jubilant	sparkling
delightful	laughing	sunny
ecstatic	light	thrilled
elated	**lively**	tickled pink
exultant	merry	up
flying high	**mirthful**	**upbeat**

CURED!

To be seventy years young is sometimes far more **cheerful** *and hopeful than to be forty years old.*

OLIVER WENDELL HOLMES JR.

My granddaughter Taevin is such a **happy** child.

In this sentence, *happy* is just too mild a word and not expressive enough to tell us the ways Taevin displays her happiness.

powerful remedies

Substitute an alternative remedy for *happy*:

My granddaughter Taevin is such a(n) _____ child.

cheerful	She is always in good spirits.
delightful	She gives us all great pleasure and delight and is very entertaining.
lively	She is full of life and vital energy—and very active.
mirthful	She is full of gladness and gaiety, so joyous.
peaceful	She is rarely argumentative or quarrelsome.
playful	She loves to play and have fun—and can find play in the simplest of things.
upbeat	She is happy, cheerful, and optimistic.

CURED!

"

*Make the expectations **lively** enough, and action will follow.*

MASON COOLEY

"

hard

PART OF SPEECH · *adjective*
DEFINITION · *difficult to do or accomplish; fatiguing; troublesome*

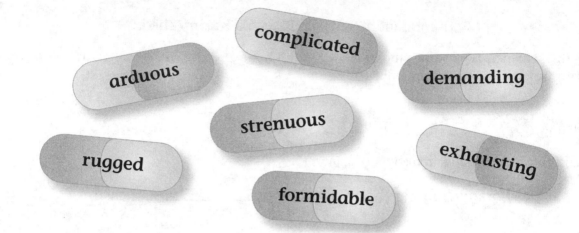

cures for the common word

arduous	harsh	**rugged**
backbreaking	heavy	scabrous
ball-breaking	herculean	serious
bothersome	intricate	severe
burdensome	involved	slavish
complex	irksome	sticky
complicated	knotty	**strenuous**
demanding	laborious	terrible
distressing	mean	tiring
exacting	merciless	toilsome
exhausting	murderous	tough
fatiguing	onerous	troublesome
formidable	operose	unsparing
grinding	rigorous	wearing
hairy	rough	wearisome

*In ballet a **complicated** story is impossible to tell. . . . We can't dance synonyms.*

GEORGE BALANCHINE

DIAGNOSIS *vague*

> The **hard** hike up Mount Tam took us the whole day.

We can't tell from the use of *hard* if the hike was more than we would have hoped for or a welcome challenge.

powerful remedies

Substitute an alternative remedy for *hard*:

> The _____ hike up Mount Tam took us the whole day.

arduous	The hike was laborious and steep and required great exertion.
complicated	The hike had aspects that were elaborate, complex, and intricate.
demanding	The hike called for more intensive effort, attention, and skill than we expected.
exhausting	By the end of the hike, we were extremely fatigued and weary.
formidable	The hike proved to be somewhat discouraging because of Mount Tam's intimidating size and difficulty.
rugged	The terrain was rocky or hilly, with jagged surfaces.
strenuous	The hike was characterized by vigorous exertion, but the connotation is that it was a positive and enjoyable workout.

CURED!

*Golf seems to be an **arduous** way to go for a walk. I prefer to take the dogs out.*

PRINCESS ANNE

help

PART OF SPEECH   *verb*

DEFINITION   *to give aid; to be of service or advantage; to assist*

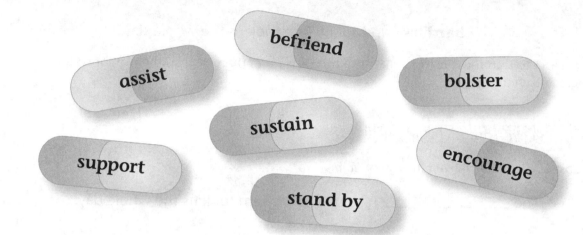

assist   befriend   bolster   sustain   support   encourage   stand by

cures for the common word

abet	cooperate	relieve
accommodate	**encourage**	root for
advocate	endorse	sanction
aid	further	save
assist	intercede	second
back	maintain	serve
ballyhoo	open doors	**stand by**
befriend	patronize	stimulate
benefit	plug	stump for
bolster	promote	succor
boost	prop	**support**
buck up	puff	**sustain**
cheer	push	uphold

CURED!

*We all of us need assistance. Those who **sustain** others themselves want to be sustained.*

MAURICE HULST

DIAGNOSIS *vague*

> Helga was kind enough to **help** me through a tough time.

Help can come in many ways, and *help* doesn't tell us much about the ways Helga's showed her kindness.

powerful remedies

Substitute an alternative remedy for *help*:

> Helga was kind enough to _____ me through a tough time.

assist	Helga offered me aid—financially, emotionally, and in other ways.
befriend	Helga and I weren't as close before this tough time, and now she's become much more friendly.
bolster	I was a little shaky, and Helga offered me her strength—she was someone to lean on.
encourage	Helga has inspired me with courage, spirit, and confidence.
stand by	Even when things got really rough, I knew I could rely on Helga.
support	Helga not only offered me financial aid but also held me up emotionally.
sustain	Helga helped me keep going without either of us giving way or yielding to how tough the time was.

*A government that robs Peter to pay Paul can always depend on the **support** of Paul.*

GEORGE BERNARD SHAW

important

| PART OF SPEECH | *adjective* |
| DEFINITION | *substantial; of much or great significance or consequence* |

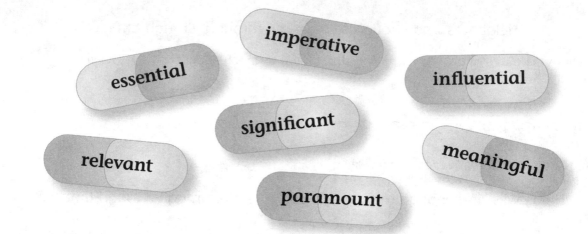

cures for the common word

big-league	grave	ponderous
chief	great	pressing
considerable	heavy	primary
conspicuous	**imperative**	principal
critical	importunate	**relevant**
crucial	**influential**	salient
decisive	large	serious
earnest	marked	signal
essential	material	**significant**
exceptional	**meaningful**	something
exigent	momentous	standout
extensive	notable	substantial
far-reaching	of note	urgent
foremost	of substance	vital
front-page	**paramount**	weighty

*Only Irish Coffee provides in a single glass all four **essential** food groups: alcohol, caffeine, sugar, fat.*

ALEX LEVINE

Community approval of the new clinic is **important** to the developer.

We can't tell from the use of *important* in this sentence if the approval is something the developer cares about or if it's required for construction of the new clinic.

powerful remedies

Substitute an alternative remedy for *important*:

Community approval of the new clinic is _____ to the developer.

essential	The approval is necessary to the actual continuance of the project, and without it, the project will not move forward.
imperative	In addition to being absolutely necessary or required, the community's input is unavoidable.
influential	The community's input will influence the developer's plans.
meaningful	This gives the impression that the developer cares about the wishes of the community.
paramount	The community's approval could have a chief impact on the developer's plans.
relevant	The community's input should have significant and demonstrable bearing on the issues.
significant	The community's approval matters, but there's no indication the approval—or not—will have any bearing on the developer's plan.

*The most **influential** of all educational factors is the conversation in a child's home.*

WILLIAM TEMPLE

interesting

PART OF SPEECH	*adjective*
DEFINITION	*arousing the curiosity or engaging the attention*

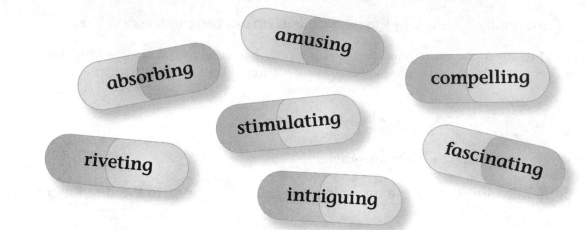

cures for the common word

absorbing	engrossing	magnetic
affecting	entertaining	pleasing
alluring	enthralling	pleasurable
amusing	entrancing	provocative
arresting	exceptional	refreshing
captivating	exotic	**riveting**
charismatic	**fascinating**	**stimulating**
compelling	gracious	stirring
curious	gripping	striking
delightful	impressive	suspicious
elegant	inspiring	thought-provoking
enchanting	**intriguing**	unusual
engaging	inviting	winning

CURED!

*I enjoyed the courtroom as a stage—but not so **amusing** as Broadway.*

MAE WEST

DIAGNOSIS   *vague*

My mom and I saw a very **interesting** play.

It is hard to know exactly what this means—if the play was good, bad, or something else entirely.

Substitute an alternative remedy for *interesting*:

My mom and I saw a very _____ play.

absorbing	The play was engaging and engrossing and occupied our full attention or interest.
amusing	The play was entertaining in a light, playful, or pleasant manner and caused us to laugh.
compelling	The play irresistibly kept our attention and urged, almost forced, us to think about its message.
fascinating	The play was irresistibly charming and captivating and caused us to see a point with a different perspective.
intriguing	The play aroused our interest—and our curiosity.
riveting	The play held our attention and kept us engrossed in the action, dialogue, or message.
stimulating	The play was exciting and invigorating.

*Good communication is as **stimulating** as black coffee, and just as hard to sleep after.*

ANNE MORROW LINDBERGH

keep

PART OF SPEECH	*verb*
DEFINITION	*to hold or retain in one's possession*

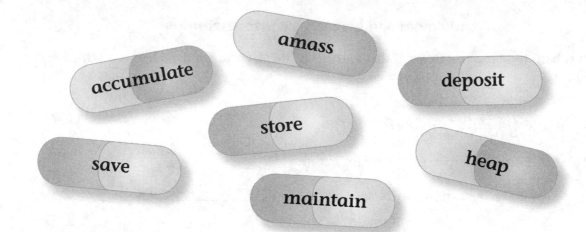

cures for the common word

accumulate	enjoy	place
amass	garner	possess
cache	grasp	preserve
care for	grip	put up
carry	have	reserve
conduct	**heap**	retain
conserve	hold back	**save**
control	**maintain**	stack
deposit	manage	stock
detain	own	**store**
direct	pile	withhold

*We **accumulate** our opinions at an age when our understanding is at its weakest.*

G. C. (GEORG CHRISTOPH) LICHTENBERG

> There's room for Chris to **keep** his entire antique ski collection in the new garage.

In this sentence, *keep* doesn't tell us precisely what Chris is doing with the collection and what the main advantage is of the new garage.

powerful remedies

Substitute an alternative remedy for *keep*:

> There's room for Chris to _____ his entire antique ski collection in the new garage.

accumulate   Chris will be able to collect his skis in gradual degrees.

amass   Chris will have plenty of room to collect a large quantity of his skis.

deposit   Choosing *deposit* implies that it's not Chris's garage, but that someone is letting Chris leave his collection there.

heap   Chris is going to pile up his collection in the garage.

maintain   The new garage gives Chris a place to work on and keep his collection in good condition.

save   Chris's collection will now be safe in the new garage.

store   Chris may not get to enjoy his collection all the time, but now he can place it in the new garage for future use.

*It is possible to **store** the mind with a million facts and still be entirely uneducated.*

ALEC BOURNE

kind

PART OF SPEECH	*adjective*
DEFINITION	*of a good or benevolent nature or disposition*

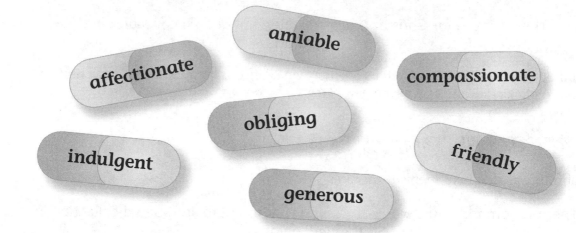

cures for the common word

affectionate	considerate	lenient
all heart	cordial	loving
altruistic	courteous	mild
amiable	**friendly**	neighborly
amicable	**generous**	**obliging**
beneficent	gentle	philanthropic
benevolent	good-hearted	propitious
big	gracious	softhearted
bounteous	humane	sympathetic
charitable	humanitarian	tenderhearted
clement	**indulgent**	thoughtful
compassionate	kindhearted	tolerant
congenial	kindly	understanding

Always when I see a man fond of praise I always think it is because he is an **affectionate** *man craving for affection.*

J. B. YEATS

Everyone likes the **kind** nanny.

There are many facets of being *kind*, and the following alternatives tell us more about the different ways in which she might be a great nanny.

Substitute an alternative remedy for *kind*:

Everyone likes the _____ nanny.

affectionate	She shows love and affection and is fondly tender.
amiable	She is very agreeable and willing to accept the wishes, decisions, or suggestions of others.
compassionate	She is sympathetic and feels and shows compassion.
friendly	She is kind and pleasant, not antagonistic or hostile.
generous	She is unselfish and liberal in giving and sharing—of her time, creativity, and attention.
indulgent	She's lenient and permissive; *indulgent* carries a somewhat negative connotation of her giving in too much.
obliging	She is often willing or eager to do favors for people and is very accommodating.

*Conrad Hilton was very **generous** to me in the divorce settlement. He gave me 5,000 Gideon Bibles.*

ZSA ZSA GABOR

know

PART OF SPEECH	*verb*
DEFINITION	*to perceive or understand as fact or truth; to apprehend clearly and with certainty*

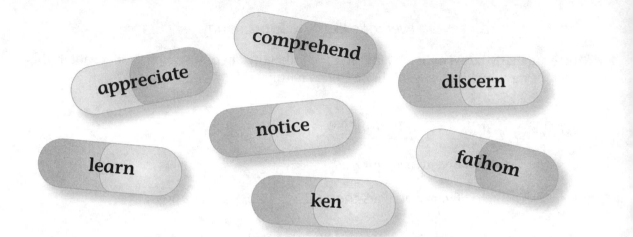

cures for the common word

apperceive	**comprehend**	have
appreciate	differentiate	**ken**
apprehend	**discern**	**learn**
be acquainted	discriminate	**notice**
be cognizant	distinguish	perceive
be informed	experience	realize
be read	**fathom**	recognize
be versed	feel certain	see
cognize	grasp	understand

> *The movies are so rarely great art, that if we can't **appreciate** great trash, there is little reason for us to go.*
>
> PAULINE KAEL

It took me a while to **know** the local customs.

Being familiar with local customs can be very helpful, but this sentence doesn't clearly indicate whether I understand or accept the customs.

powerful remedies

Substitute an alternative remedy for *know*:

It took me a while to _____ the local customs.

appreciate
I became fully aware of the customs and was able to acknowledge that they are true for the area.

comprehend
Even though some of the customs were unfamiliar to me, I grasped their nature and meaning.

discern
By observing, I became able to recognize certain actions as local customs—as opposed to unfamiliar individual behavior.

fathom
I was finally able to comprehend and perceive the truth of the customs.

ken
I was already acquainted with some of the customs, because someone had told me about some of them, and now I understand them even more.

learn
I came to know about the customs from my own study and experience.

notice
It took me a while even to become aware of the local customs.

CURED!

Learn from the mistakes of others—you can never live long enough to make them all yourself.

JOHN LUTHER

leave

PART OF SPEECH	*verb*
DEFINITION	*to depart from permanently; to quit*

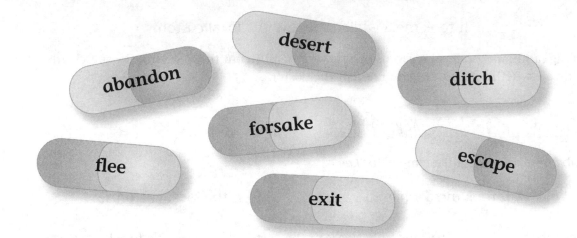

abandon · *desert* · *ditch* · *forsake* · *flee* · *escape* · *exit*

cures for the common word

abandon	**flee**	ride off
abscond	flit	run along
break away	fly	sally
cast off	**forsake**	scram
clear out	go away	set out
cut out	go forth	slip out
decamp	head out	split
defect	migrate	step down
desert	move out	take leave
disappear	part	take off
ditch	pull out	vacate
embark	push off	vamoose
emigrate	quit	vanish
escape	relinquish	walk out
exit	retire	withdraw

CURED!

*A poem is never finished, only **abandoned**.*

PAUL VALERY

> Darrel had to **leave** his car at the side of the road.

No doubt there was something wrong for Darrel to have to leave his car, but *leave* in this sentence doesn't give an indication of just why, and the following alternatives tell a bit more of the story.

powerful remedies

Substitute an alternative remedy for *leave*:

> Darrel had to _____ his car at the side of the road.

abandon	Darrel needed to leave and completely give up on the car, which was perhaps broken beyond repair.
desert	Darrel left the car without intending to return; the implication is that he left contrary to a promise or commitment not to.
ditch	This is an informal way to say that Darrel had to get rid of the car for some reason.
escape	Darrel got away from the car—after being confined or restrained in it for some reason—perhaps because of some impending danger.
exit	Darrel gave up possession of the car; the implication is that he was able to walk away calmly as opposed to hurrying away.
flee	Darrel quickly ran away from the car, but we still don't know why.
forsake	Darrel adored that classic car, but for some reason he sadly had to give it up.

*Nobody grows old merely by living a number of years. We grow old by **deserting** our ideals. Years may wrinkle the skin, but to give up enthusiasm wrinkles the soul.*

SAMUEL ULLMAN

PART OF SPEECH   *noun*
DEFINITION   *the way in which a person or thing appears to the eye or to the mind*

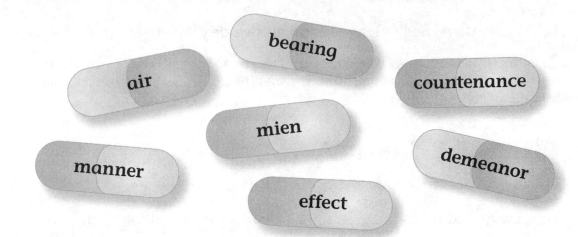

air
bearing
countenance
mien
demeanor
manner
effect

cures for the common word

air	**effect**	**mien**
aspect	expression	mug
attitude	face	physiognomy
bearing	fashion	posture
cast	feature	presence
character	form	seeming
complexion	guise	semblance
countenance	image	shape
demeanor	**manner**	visage

CURED!

*A man's own **manner** and character is what most becomes him.*
MARCUS TULLIUS CICERO

The woman in the park had a sad **look** about her.

In this sentence, it's unclear exactly what gave us the sense that the woman was sad, and the alternatives give us a clearer explanation of how she is demonstrating her sadness.

powerful remedies

Substitute an alternative remedy for *look*:

The woman in the park had a sad _____ about her.

air
It was her appearance or manner that gave the impression of being sad.

bearing
Her posture and the way she conducted herself, maybe even her gestures, made her appear sad.

countenance
The look or expression on her face was sad.

demeanor
Her conduct and behavior—perhaps crying—told us she was sad.

effect
By her look or manner, she was causing those around her to be sad.

manner
The way she was speaking with and treating others told us of her sadness.

mien
Some aspect of her manner revealed her inner state of sadness.

CURED!

*Excess on occasion is exhilarating. It prevents moderation from acquiring the deadening **effect** of a habit.*

W. SOMERSET MAUGHAM

love

PART OF SPEECH	*noun*
DEFINITION	*a profoundly tender, passionate affection for another person or an object*

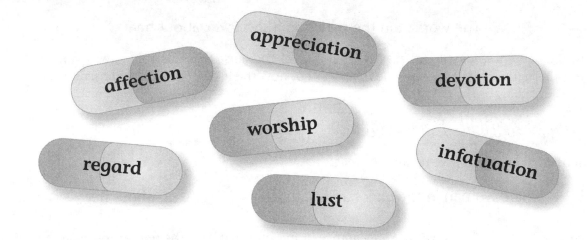

cures for the common word

adulation	enjoyment	passion
affection	fervor	rapture
allegiance	fidelity	**regard**
amity	fondness	relish
amour	friendship	respect
appreciation	hankering	sentiment
ardor	idolatry	soft spot
attachment	inclination	taste
crush	**infatuation**	tenderness
delight	involvement	weakness
devotion	liking	**worship**
emotion	**lust**	yearning
enchantment	partiality	zeal

*After a semester or so, my **infatuation** with computers burnt out as quickly as it had begun.*

ERIC ALLIN CORNELL

Taylor realized that her feelings for Thorne were actually **love**.

Love can have a broad spectrum of meanings, and in this sentence, *love* doesn't give us much clarity on the level of Taylor's feelings.

powerful remedies

Substitute an alternative remedy for *love*:

Taylor realized that her feelings for Thorne were actually _____.

affection   Taylor had a tender fondness for Thorne, but it wasn't really true love.

appreciation   Taylor felt great gratitude to Thorne, but not necessarily an affection for him.

devotion   Taylor was thankful to Thorne to a degree that caused an earnest attachment to him.

infatuation   Taylor had a foolish, all-absorbing passion for Thorne, which probably won't last.

lust   Taylor realized she really only had an intense sexual desire for Thorne.

regard   Taylor had great respect for Thorne and held him in high esteem.

worship   Taylor had an adoring reverence for Thorne.

CURED!

*Perpetual **devotion** to what a man calls his business, is only to be sustained by perpetual neglect of many other things.*

ROBERT LOUIS STEVENSON

PART OF SPEECH	adjective
DEFINITION	chief in size, extent, or importance; principal; leading

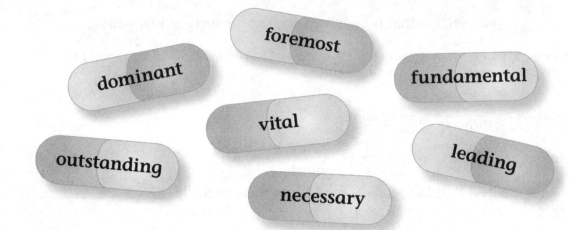

cures for the common word

capital	**foremost**	preeminent
cardinal	**fundamental**	premier
central	head	prevailing
chief	**leading**	primary
controlling	major	prime
critical	**necessary**	special
crucial	**outstanding**	star
dominant	paramount	stellar
essential	particular	supreme
first	predominant	**vital**

*Start by doing what is **necessary**, then do what is possible, and suddenly you are doing the impossible.*

SAINT FRANCIS OF ASSISI

DIAGNOSIS   *vague*

The article's **main** point concerned increased global warming.

We know that *main* implies importance of some kind, but we're not sure in what way or on what the importance is based.

 powerful remedies

Substitute an alternative remedy for *main*:

The article's _____ point concerned increased global warming.

dominant
There were many points in the article, and increased global warming is the one that most influenced the information or perspective of the article.

foremost
Increased global warming was the article's most important point, ahead of all others.

fundamental
Increased global warming was the primary point upon which the rest of the article was based.

leading
Increased global warming was the first point of the article.

necessary
The point of increased global warming was essential and requisite to the entire article.

outstanding
The point of increased global warming was most prominent and striking; it stood out.

vital
Getting across the truth of increased global warming was of critical importance.

*Love and freedom are **vital** to the creation and upbringing of a child.*

SYLVIA PANKHURST

make

PART OF SPEECH	*verb*
DEFINITION	*to cause to exist or happen; to bring about; to create*

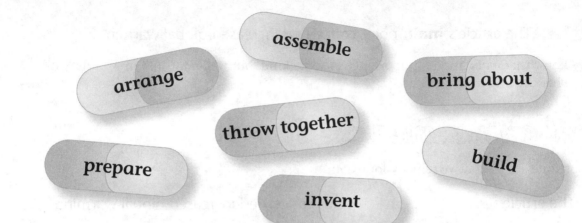

assemble

arrange

bring about

throw together

prepare

build

invent

cures for the common word

accomplish	dream up	mold
adjust	effect	occasion
arrange	engender	originate
assemble	fabricate	parent
beget	fashion	**prepare**
brew	father	procreate
bring about	forge	produce
build	form	put together
cause	frame	secure
compile	generate	shape
compose	hatch	sire
conceive	initiate	spawn
constitute	**invent**	synthesize
construct	knock out	**throw together**
cook up	manufacture	whip up

 CURED!

*The first qualification for a historian is to have no ability to **invent**.*
STENDHAL [MARIE-HENRI BEYLE]

Jason is working to **make** a state-of-the-art veterinary clinic.

This is certainly a noble cause, but *make* doesn't clearly tell us what Jason's role will be in bringing the clinic into existence.

powerful remedies

Substitute an alternative remedy for *make*:

Jason is working to _____ a state-of-the-art veterinary clinic.

arrange
Jason is bringing about an agreement to create the clinic, but we don't know if he will be involved with putting together the clinic.

assemble
Jason is going to bring together all the components needed for the entire clinic.

bring about
This is an informal way to say that Jason will do everything necessary to accomplish the goal of bringing the clinic into existence.

build
This could mean that Jason will actually help to construct the building, but it may mean that he will be instrumental in assembling all the parts needed to establish the clinic.

invent
This implies there has never been such a clinic and Jason is creating it based on his own ingenuity—and maybe some experimentation.

prepare
This implies a clinic is in existence and Jason is going to be sure it is duly state-of-the-art equipped in proper condition and readiness.

throw together
Jason is putting together the clinic in a hurried way, and although this can have a connotation of being haphazard, in today's world it can imply admiration for doing something so big so quickly.

CURED!

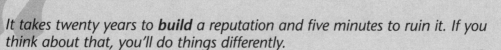

*It takes twenty years to **build** a reputation and five minutes to ruin it. If you think about that, you'll do things differently.*

WARREN BUFFET

mean

PART OF SPEECH	*adjective*
DEFINITION	*hostile, offensive, selfish, or unaccommodating; nasty; malicious*

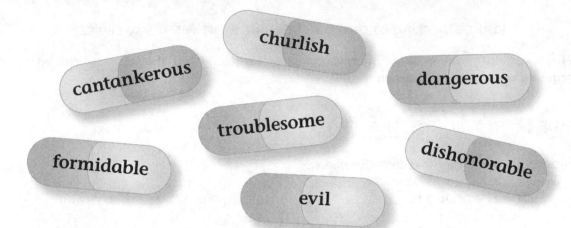

cantankerous · churlish · dangerous · formidable · troublesome · dishonorable · evil

cures for the common word

bad-tempered	hard-nosed	rugged
bitchy	ignoble	scurrilous
callous	ill-tempered	shameless
cantankerous	infamous	sinking
churlish	knavish	snide
contemptible	liverish	sour
dangerous	lousy	the lowest
despicable	malicious	treacherous
difficult	malign	**troublesome**
dirty	nasty	ugly
disagreeable	perfidious	unfriendly
dishonorable	pesky	unpleasant
evil	rotten	unscrupulous
formidable	rough	vexatious
hard	rude	vicious

CURED!

*May the forces of **evil** become confused on the way to your house.*

GEORGE CARLIN

The wicked stepmother in *Cinderella* was downright **mean**.

Well, she sure was, but *mean* is too limiting when there are so many other words to use that describe the horrid ways she showed that meanness.

powerful remedies

Substitute an alternative remedy for *mean*:

The wicked stepmother in *Cinderella* was downright _____.

cantankerous   She was constantly disagreeable and argumentative.

churlish   She was rude, crude, ill-mannered, coarse, and contemptible in behavior and appearance.

dangerous   She caused Cinderella great physical and emotional injury, to say the least.

dishonorable   She was clearly unprincipled and disreputable.

evil   Her entire personality was characterized by anger and spite.

formidable   For years she managed to cause fear and apprehension—in everyone.

troublesome   She caused trouble for everyone and was constantly annoying.

CURED!

"*Life is pleasant. Death is peaceful. It's the transition that's **troublesome**.*
                                                                    ISAAC ASIMOV"

PART OF SPEECH	*adjective*
DEFINITION	*additional or further; in greater quantity, amount, measure, degree, or number*

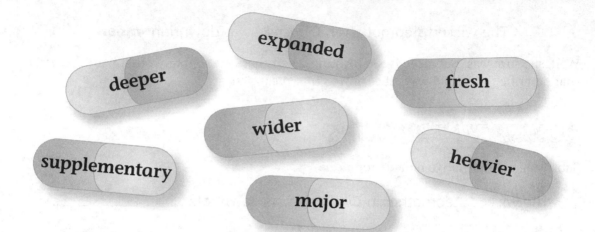

cures for the common word

added	extended	larger
additional	extra	likewise
amassed	farther	**major**
another	**fresh**	massed
augmented	further	new
bounteous	greater	numerous
deeper	**heavier**	other
enhanced	higher	replenishment
exceeding	increased	**supplementary**
expanded	innumerable	**wider**

*One should never criticize his own work except in a **fresh** and hopeful mood. The self-criticism of a tired mind is suicide.*

CHARLES HORTEN COOLEY

I need to conduct **more** research for my report.

In this sentence, *more* is clear in indicating additional research but doesn't tell us much about what kind of research.

powerful remedies

Substitute an alternative remedy for *more*:

I need to conduct _____ research for my report.

deeper
I need to continue my research extending far down from the surface meaning of my topic.

expanded
I need to look beyond the current scope of my research to increase the length and detail of my report.

fresh
I need to look at my topic in a novel and different way than I have so far.

heavier
I've been a little light on my research and need to do much more than before.

major
I haven't done any research so far, and I have a lot to do!

supplementary
I need to add something to my research to make it complete—perhaps to make up for a deficiency or to extend or strengthen the whole report.

wider
I need to look at a much greater variety of subjects or cases to give me more thorough information.

*The responsibility of tolerance lies in those who have the **wider** vision.*
GEORGE ELIOT

need

PART OF SPEECH	*noun*
DEFINITION	*urgent want, as of something required or wanted*

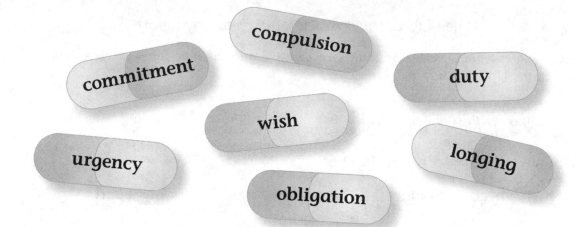

cures for the common word

ache	**duty**	requirement
charge	exigency	requisite
commitment	extremity	right
committal	hunger	thirst
compulsion	itch	urge
craving	**longing**	**urgency**
demand	must	use
desire	**obligation**	weakness
devoir	occasion	**wish**

CURED!

*I write of the **wish** that comes true—for some reason, a terrifying concept.*

JAMES M. CAIN

Parents may feel a **need** to protect even their adult children.

In this sentence, *need* doesn't give us a clear indication as to whether the desire to protect is appropriate or not.

powerful remedies

Substitute an alternative remedy for *need*:

Parents may feel a _____ to protect even their adult children.

commitment   Parents may feel bound emotionally to protect their children with a sincere and steadfast pledge, which tends to give us a positive sense.

compulsion   Some parents have an irresistible impulse to protect their children, regardless of the rationality of the motivation; *compulsion* tells us that the feeling is probably not appropriate.

duty   Parents may feel they are doing what they are required to do by moral or legal obligation.

longing   Some parents have a strong, persistent desire or craving to protect their adult children.

obligation   Parents may feel bound by duty, custom, or law to protect their children; the connotation is that perhaps they are doing so because they *have to* rather than because they *want to*.

urgency   There may be an earnest and pressing importance for the parents to protect their children; the implication is that there is real danger.

wish   Parents often have a continuing want and desire to protect their children.

*The **duty** of youth is to challenge corruption.*

KURT COBAIN

new

PART OF SPEECH	*adjective*
DEFINITION	*of recent origin, production, purchase, etc.*

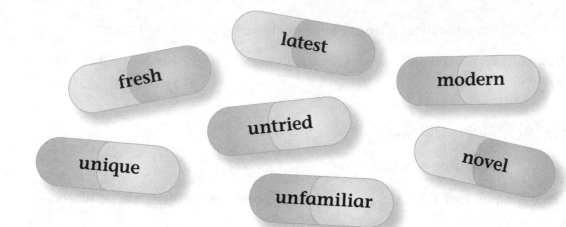

fresh latest modern unique untried novel unfamiliar

cures for the common word

dewy
different
dissimilar
distinct
edgy
fashionable
fresh
inexperienced
just out
latest
modern
modernistic
modish

neoteric
newfangled
novel
now
original
recent
strange
topical
ultramodern
uncontaminated
unfamiliar
unique
unknown

unlike
unseasoned
unskilled
unspoiled
untouched
untrained
untried
untrodden
unused
unusual
up-to-date
virgin
youthful

CURED!

*I think **modern** science should graft functional wings on a pig, simply so no one can ever use that stupid saying again.*

ANONYMOUS

The detergent manufacturer introduced a **new** formula.

In this example, *new* could have a host of different meanings—both positive and negative.

powerful remedies

Substitute an alternative remedy for *new*:

The detergent manufacturer introduced a _____ formula.

fresh	The formula is newly made or obtained.
latest	The formula may have been created at any time, and this is the most recent formula the manufacturer is introducing.
modern	The formula is characteristic or expressive of recent times.
novel	The formula is of a new kind, different from anything seen or known before.
unfamiliar	The formula may have been around for some time but is not known or well known.
unique	This could have two slightly different meanings: the formula is the only one of its kind, or it is not the typical formula.
untried	The formula possibly has not ever been tried or at least has not been adequately tested or proved.

*Create your own visual style . . . let it be **unique** for yourself and yet identifiable for others.*

GEORGE ORSON WELLES

next

PART OF SPEECH   *adjective*
DEFINITION   *immediately following in time, order, importance, etc.*

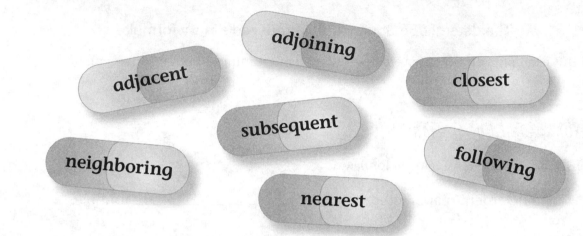

cures for the common word

abutting	**closest**	later
adjacent	coming	nearby
adjoining	connecting	**nearest**
after	consecutive	**neighboring**
alongside	consequent	proximate
attached	contiguous	**subsequent**
beside	ensuing	succeeding
bordering	**following**	thereafter
close	immediate	touching

CURED!

*Arrogance and snobbism live in **adjoining** rooms and use a common currency.*

MORLEY SAFER

Rosie's best friend lives in Brewster, the **next** town on Highway 1.

Choosing *next* here actually gives us sufficient information, but the following alternatives broaden our understanding of where Brewster is in relation to where Rosie lives.

powerful remedies

Substitute an alternative remedy for *next*:

Rosie's best friend lives in Brewster, the _____ town on Highway 1.

adjacent
Brewster is close to Rosie's town, but *adjacent* doesn't give us an indication of in which direction or if it's a bordering town or simply nearby.

adjoining
Brewster is bordering the town where Rosie lives, in direct contact at some point.

closest
There are several towns nearby, but Brewster is most near to Rosie's town.

following
Continuing on Highway 1, Brewster is a town we'll come to—though it doesn't tell us how close or in which direction.

nearest
Brewster is within the shortest distance or interval of time from Rosie's house.

neighboring
Since we're talking of towns, this is an ideal word for a nearby or adjacent town.

subsequent
On Highway 1, Brewster is the town that comes after Rosie's town—again, though, it doesn't tell us in which direction or how far it is.

CURED!

At a formal dinner party, the person nearest death should always be seated **closest** *to the bathroom.*

GEORGE CARLIN

nice

PART OF SPEECH *adjective*
DEFINITION *pleasing and agreeable in nature*

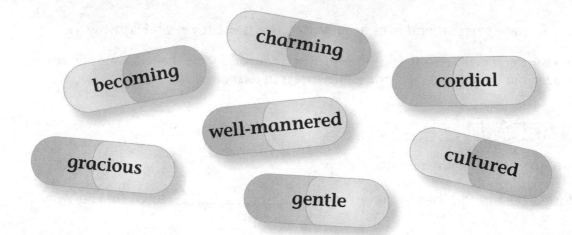

becoming

charming

cordial

well-mannered

gracious

cultured

gentle

cures for the common word

admirable	delightful	nifty
agreeable	favorable	obliging
amiable	friendly	OK
approved	genial	peachy
attractive	**gentle**	pleasant
becoming	good	pleasurable
charming	**gracious**	polite
commendable	helpful	seemly
considerate	hunky-dory	swell
copacetic	ingratiating	unpresumptuous
cordial	inviting	welcome
courteous	kind	**well-mannered**
cultured	kindly	winning
decorous	lovely	winsome

CURED!

*Being **cultured** is the least expensive form of respectability.*

MASON COOLEY

Rich has a **nice** personality.

We know that this means something positive (unless being used facetiously), but we'd like to know more precisely what is pleasant about Rich.

Substitute an alternative remedy for *nice*:

Rich has a(n) _____ personality.

becoming
Rich's personality is pleasing and appropriate, and he presents himself in the best light.

charming
Rich is a delight and can induce an action using his strong attractiveness or personal skills.

cordial
Rich is warm, sincere, and friendly.

cultured
Rich is refined in his manner and enlightened and knowledgeable in the arts.

gentle
Rich is never severe or harsh in any way.

gracious
Rich is kind and courteous and has a compassionate nature.

well-mannered
Rich is polite and courteous and is considered to be socially "correct" in his behavior.

*I'm a **charming** coward; I fight with words.*

CARL REINER

old

PART OF SPEECH	*adjective*
DEFINITION	*having lived or existed for a relatively long time; far advanced in years or life*

experienced

aged

mature

veteran

seasoned

skilled

senior

cures for the common word

aged	geriatric	**seasoned**
ancient	getting on	senile
broken down	gray-haired	**senior**
debilitated	grizzled	**skilled**
decrepit	hoary	superannuated
deficient	impaired	tired
doddering	inactive	used
elderly	infirm	venerable
enfeebled	**mature**	versed
exhausted	matured	**veteran**
experienced	olden	wasted
fossil	patriarchal	worn

CURED!

*Imagination grows by exercise, and contrary to common belief, is more powerful in the **mature** than in the young.*

W. SOMERSET MAUGHAM

DIAGNOSIS *vague*

Jim is an **old** member of the cast.

When *old* is used in this context, it would probably be kinder to look for an alternative—one that has a more diplomatic and more precise connotation.

powerful remedies

Substitute an alternative remedy for *old*:

Jim is a(n) _____ member of the cast.

aged

We don't know how long Jim has been with the cast, but he is advanced in age.

experienced

Whether it's with this cast or just in the industry, Jim has gained a level of skill or knowledge based on his past experience.

mature

Jim—or at least his skills—are fully developed in body or mind.

seasoned

Jim is competent because of his trial and experience.

senior

Though this could relate to Jim's chronological age, it would more often imply he is of higher or the highest rank or standing in the cast.

skilled

Jim's skill is either from experience or from training.

veteran

Jim has long service with the cast.

CURED!

*I was very, very naive for a **veteran** guy. I thought I was going to be a place where dissent could be heard.*

PHIL DONAHUE

old

PART OF SPEECH   *adjective*
DEFINITION   *obsolete; no longer in general use*

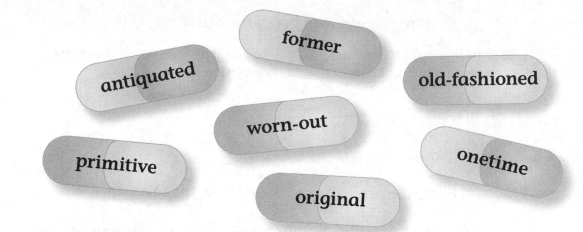

antiquated · former · old-fashioned · worn-out · primitive · onetime · original

cures for the common word

aboriginal	hackneyed	previous
age-old	immemorial	primeval
antediluvian	late	**primitive**
antiquated	moth-eaten	primordial
antique	of yore	quondam
archaic	olden	remote
bygone	oldfangled	rusty
cast-off	**old-fashioned**	stale
crumbling	old-time	superannuated
dated	**onetime**	time-worn
decayed	**original**	traditional
démodéd	outdated	unfashionable
early	outmoded	unoriginal
erstwhile	passé	venerable
former	past	**worn-out**

CURED!

*An **original** writer is not one who imitates nobody, but one whom nobody can imitate.*

FRANÇOIS-RENÉ DE CHATEAUBRIAND

The manuscript files are on my **old** computer.

For a second printing of my book, I need the original manuscript files, and we can't tell from the use of *old* in this sentence whether I'm going to be able to get those files or not.

powerful remedies

Substitute an alternative remedy for *old*:

The manuscript files are on my _____ computer.

antiquated	The files are on a computer that is so obsolete I no longer use it.
former	I'm referring to the computer I used before my current one, and it doesn't necessarily mean there was or is anything wrong with it.
old-fashioned	The computer is out of style but still may work just fine.
onetime	The connotation is that the files are on the computer I used at one time and may no longer have access to.
original	The files are on my very first computer.
primitive	The computer is rather simple and unsophisticated and probably can't even perform the way I need it to today.
worn-out	My beloved computer is no longer working; it is so damaged by use that it's beyond repair.

Only two things are infinite, the universe and human stupidity, and I'm not sure about the ***former****.*

ALBERT EINSTEIN

open

PART OF SPEECH	*adjective*
DEFINITION	*not closed or barred; relatively free of obstructions*

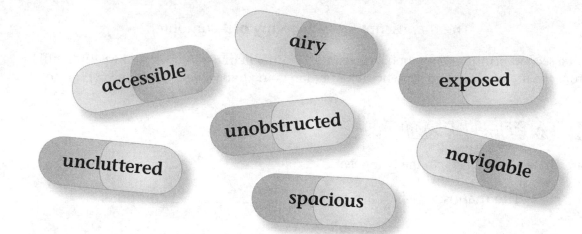

cures for the common word

accessible	gaping	unbolted
agape	naked	unburdened
airy	**navigable**	**uncluttered**
ajar	patent	uncovered
bare	patulous	unfolded
clear	peeled	unfurled
cleared	revealed	unimpeded
dehiscent	rolling	unlocked
disclosed	**spacious**	**unobstructed**
emptied	spread out	unsealed
expansive	stripped	unstopped
exposed	susceptible	vacated
extended	unbarred	wide
free	unblocked	yawning

*We're an ideal political family, as **accessible** as Disneyland.*

MAUREEN REAGAN

> We're creating an **open** path from the house to the garden.

Because *open* as an adjective has almost eighty definitions, many of which could apply in this sentence, we definitely need to narrow our meaning to have a clearer picture about the path to the garden.

powerful remedies

Substitute an alternative remedy for *open*:

> We're creating a(n) _____ path from the house to the garden.

accessible   We'll now have a path that can be easily reached and used.

airy   The path may be covered, but it is open to a free current of fresh air.

exposed   The path won't be sheltered from the elements.

navigable   The path will now be wide enough to provide us easy passage to the garden.

spacious   Our path will have a great vast area.

uncluttered   The path now will be orderly and neat.

unobstructed   We're clearing any and all impediments or hindrances to create a clear path.

*I would rather be **exposed** to the inconveniences attending too much liberty than to those attending too small a degree of it.*

THOMAS JEFFERSON

part

PART OF SPEECH   *noun*
DEFINITION   *a portion or division of a whole that is separate or distinct*

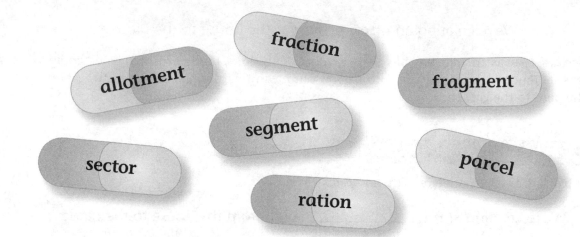

cures for the common word

allotment	helping	piece
apportionment	hunk	portion
articulation	ingredient	quantum
bit	installment	**ration**
branch	item	scrap
chunk	limb	section
component	lot	**sector**
constituent	measure	**segment**
department	member	share
detail	module	side
division	moiety	slice
element	molecule	sliver
factor	organ	splinter
fraction	**parcel**	subdivision
fragment	particle	unit

*To me, photography is the simultaneous recognition, in a **fraction** of a second, of the significance of an event.*

HENRI CARTIER-BRESSON

DIAGNOSIS *vague*

A **part** of the population was evacuated early.

In this sentence, we aren't given enough information to know how many people were evacuated or if the early evacuation was a positive or negative situation.

Substitute an alternative remedy for *part*:

A(n) _____ of the population was evacuated early.

allotment A predetermined number of people, or specific people, had been chosen for early evacuation should the need arise.

fraction Only a minute number of people were evacuated early, and in this case, the implication is that the number was far too few.

fragment Only a small, isolated group of people were evacuated early.

parcel The people in a specific geographic portion of the city were evacuated early; *parcel* implies a relatively small geographic area.

ration Only a set amount of people were set apart for early evacuation; the implication with *ration* is that it was a small number of people.

sector A geographic section or zone of the population was evacuated early, though we have no indication how small or large that section was.

segment Though *segment* could refer to a geographic location, the connotation is more that a certain group determined by some other factor (perhaps need or, unfortunately, economic status) was evacuated early.

*It is unconscionable that we **ration** health care by the ability to pay. . . . Your heart breaks. Health care should be a given.*

KATHRYN ANASTOS

perfect

PART OF SPEECH	*adjective*
DEFINITION	*entirely without any flaws, defects, or shortcomings*

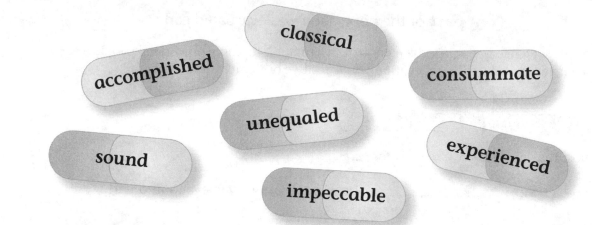

cures for the common word

absolute	faultless	skillful
accomplished	finished	**sound**
aces	flawless	splendid
adept	foolproof	spotless
beyond compare	ideal	stainless
blameless	immaculate	sublime
classical	**impeccable**	superb
consummate	indefectible	supreme
crowning	masterful	ten
culminating	masterly	unblemished
defectless	matchless	**unequaled**
excellent	paradisiacal	unmarred
excelling	peerless	untainted
experienced	pure	untarnished
expert	skilled	utopian

CURED!

*The advantage of a **classical** education is that it enables you to despise the wealth which it prevents you from achieving.*

RUSSELL GREEN

Susan is a **perfect** first-chair violinist.

Susan is an ideal choice, but this doesn't give us much information as to what specifically makes her so right for the position.

powerful remedies

Substitute an alternative remedy for *perfect*:

Susan is a(n) _____ first-chair violinist.

accomplished	Susan is highly skilled as a violinist; she is an expert.
classical	*Classical* in this sentence could have two meanings: Susan's talents are of the highest quality, or she plays more enduring types of music.
consummate	Susan can superbly perform a complete range of music.
experienced	Susan is certainly skillful through her experience, but this may refer instead to her experience at being first chair.
impeccable	Susan's playing is considered faultless.
sound	Susan is competent and reliable, which may be fine but doesn't indicate an advanced skill.
unequaled	Susan's talents as a violinist are matchless and cannot be surpassed.

*John Wayne was a **consummate** gentleman. Bigger than life.*

JENNIFER O'NEILL

piece

PART OF SPEECH	*noun*
DEFINITION	*a separate or limited portion or quantity of something*

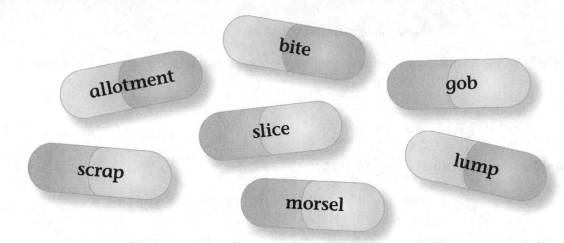

cures for the common word

allotment	hunk	portion
bit	instance	quantity
bite	interest	quota
case	item	sample
chomp	length	**scrap**
chunk	lot	section
cut	**lump**	segment
division	member	share
example	moiety	shred
fraction	**morsel**	**slice**
fragment	mouthful	smithereens
gob	parcel	snack
half	percentage	specimen

*Sculpture is the art of the hole and the **lump**.*

AUGUSTE RODIN

DIAGNOSIS *vague*

When I got home from work, I saw that the family had left me one **piece** of pie.

In this sentence, I'm not sure just how big—or small—a *piece* of pie I'm going to get to enjoy.

Substitute an alternative remedy for *piece*:

When I got home from work, I saw that the family had left me one _____ of pie.

allotment   There are five in the family and five pieces of pie, so they kindly set aside my equal share.

bite   Well, it's not a lot, but at least they left a mouthful.

gob   Using *gob* here is an informal way to say they left me a huge quantity of pie.

lump   It was an irregularly shaped mass on the plate, so they probably had all picked away at it.

morsel   There was such a small portion left, I could barely get a good taste.

scrap   Unfortunately, all that was left were bits and pieces of leftovers.

slice   Ah, a standard cut of pie—in this case big enough to enjoy fully.

CURED!

*Right now, I'm as single as a **slice** of American cheese.*

NICK CANNON

plain

PART OF SPEECH	*adjective*
DEFINITION	*straightforward; frank or candid*

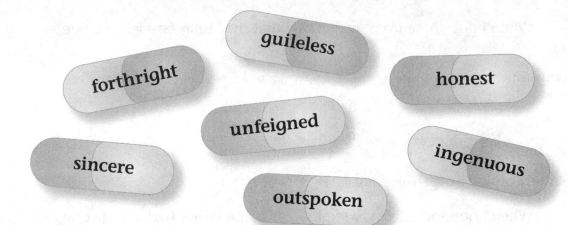

forthright

guileless

honest

unfeigned

sincere

ingenuous

outspoken

cures for the common word

abrupt	**guileless**	straightforward
artless	**honest**	true
blunt	impolite	unconcealed
candid	**ingenuous**	undisguised
direct	open	**unfeigned**
downright	**outspoken**	uninhibited
forthright	rude	unreserved
frank	**sincere**	unrestricted
genuine	straight arrow	unvarnished

CURED!

Honest criticism is hard to take, particularly from a relative, a friend, an acquaintance, or a stranger.

FRANKLIN P. JONES

DIAGNOSIS   *vague*

Robert is known for his **plain** speaking.

We can't be sure what's meant by *plain* here nor whether Robert's speaking style is considered positive or negative.

powerful remedies

Substitute an alternative remedy for *plain*:

Robert is known for his _____ speaking.

forthright   Robert goes straight to the point, without any subtlety or evasion.

guileless   What Robert says is free of deceit.

honest   Robert always speaks with honorable, upright, and fair intentions.

ingenuous   Robert speaks sincerely and without reservation.

outspoken   This means Robert speaks with frankness and without reservation, but *outspoken* has a connotation that this may be unwelcome or may be considered inappropriate.

sincere   Robert speaks in a genuine and earnest way—with the added connotation that he speaks with emotion.

unfeigned   Robert is genuine and says what he sincerely feels.

CURED!

"*I can see clearly now . . . that I was wrong in not acting more decisively and more* **forthrightly** *in dealing with Watergate.*"

RICHARD M. NIXON

plan

PART OF SPEECH	*noun*
DEFINITION	*a scheme or method of acting, doing, proceeding, making, etc.*

cures for the common word

aim	intendment	project
angle	intention	proposal
animus	layout	proposition
arrangement	machination	purpose
big picture	means	scenario
contrivance	**method**	scheme
deal	outline	**stratagem**
design	pattern	**strategy**
device	picture	suggestion
disposition	**platform**	system
expedient	plot	tactic
game plan	policy	treatment
gimmick	procedure	undertaking
idea	program	way

*Art and science have their meeting point in **method**.*
EDWARD ROBERT BULWER-LYTTON

For his extreme-sports training start-up company, Sam considered a bold marketing **plan**.

We expect something in a field like extreme sports to be bold, and the alternatives give us a much better feel for what Sam wants to accomplish with his marketing.

powerful remedies

Substitute an alternative remedy for *plan*:

For his extreme-sports training start-up company, Sam considered a bold marketing _____.

angle	The plan is based on a certain viewpoint or attitude Sam has; *angle* can imply there is some secret motive to the plan.
game plan	Sam is considering a carefully thought-out course of action.
gimmick	Sam is considering an ingenious or novel approach designed to attract attention and increase appeal.
method	Knowing that most basics of marketing apply to all industries, Sam is considering techniques in accordance with traditional marketing procedures.
platform	Sam decided to base his approach on a body of principles in which he believes.
stratagem	Sam is thinking of an elaborate maneuver to gain an advantage over his competitors.
strategy	Sam is considering a series of maneuvers aimed at a specific goal.

CURED!

*We will never try to develop a **strategy** that wins on price. There is nothing unique about pricing.*

JOSH S. WESTON

plan

PART OF SPEECH	*verb*
DEFINITION	*to think out; to arrange a method or scheme to accomplish an objective*

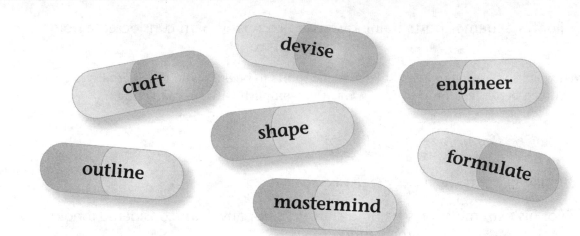

cures for the common word

arrange	**engineer**	plot
bargain for	figure out	prepare
block out	fix to	project
blueprint	form	quarterback
brainstorm	**formulate**	ready
calculate	frame	reckon on
concoct	hatch	represent
conspire	intrigue	rough in
contemplate	invent	scheme
contrive	line up	set out
cook up	map	**shape**
craft	**mastermind**	sketch
design	meditate	steer
devise	organize	trace
draft	**outline**	work out

CURED!

*A man of personality can **formulate** ideals, but only a man of character can achieve them.*

SIR HERBERT READ

The committee met to **plan** the next election campaign.

Choosing *plan* here is vague and limits our understanding of the committee's intentions.

powerful remedies

Substitute an alternative remedy for *plan*:

The committee met to _____ the next election campaign.

craft
: The committee devoted great care and ingenuity to construct a successful campaign.

devise
: The committee is aiming to elaborate on existing principles or ideas.

engineer
: The committee intends to arrange and manage the campaign by some expedient scheme, which leans toward a negative connotation.

formulate
: The committee is working to invent a method or system for a successful campaign.

mastermind
: The committee wants to skillfully plan and also direct the campaign, though *mastermind* can have a negative connotation.

outline
: The committee is in the beginning stages of summarizing and sketching out the main features of the campaign.

shape
: The committee wants to give definite form and organization to the campaign; *shape* has a positive connotation.

CURED!

*We continue to **shape** our personality all our life. If we knew ourselves perfectly, we should die.*

ALBERT CAMUS

pleasant

PART OF SPEECH   *adjective*
DEFINITION   *socially acceptable or adept; polite; amiable; agreeable*

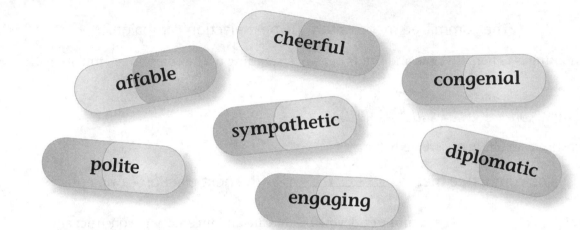

affable · cheerful · congenial · sympathetic · polite · diplomatic · engaging

cures for the common word

affable	enchanting	lovely
agreeable	**engaging**	mild-mannered
amiable	enjoyable	nice
amusing	fine	obliging
bland	friendly	pleasing
charming	fun	pleasurable
cheerful	genial	**polite**
cheery	genteel	refreshing
civilized	good-humored	satisfying
congenial	gracious	social
convivial	gratifying	soft
copacetic	jolly	sweet
cordial	jovial	**sympathetic**
delightful	kindly	urbane
diplomatic	likable	welcome

CURED!

*The most **engaging** powers of an author are to make new things familiar, familiar things new.*

WILLIAM MAKEPEACE THACKERAY

My manager, Alexa, is always **pleasant**.

What a joy to work with a pleasant manager, so using the following alternatives allow me to elaborate on the degree of her good nature.

powerful remedies

Substitute an alternative remedy for *pleasant*:

My manager, Alexa, is always _____.

affable Alexa is easy to approach and talk to, and she's warmly polite.

cheerful Alexa is always in good spirits, inspiring us to also be cheerful.

congenial Alexa is agreeable, friendly, and sociable.

diplomatic Alexa is tactful and very skilled in dealing with sensitive matters and people.

engaging Alexa is always willing to involve herself and participate—in conversations or in what needs to be done.

polite Alexa is always courteous, showing good manners toward others.

sympathetic Alexa is compassionate and shows sympathy and understanding in a wide range of issues and to many people.

CURED!

Polite conversation is rarely either.

FRAN LEBOWITZ

problem

PART OF SPEECH	*noun*
DEFINITION	*situation, matter, or person that presents perplexity or difficulty*

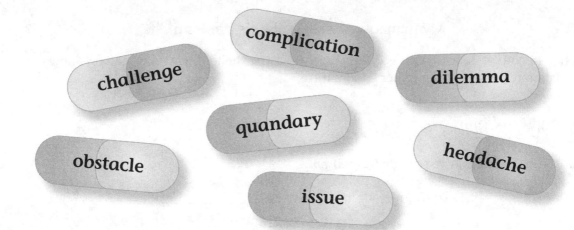

complication

challenge

dilemma

quandary

obstacle

headache

issue

cures for the common word

box	doubt	**obstacle**
challenge	**headache**	pickle
complication	hitch	predicament
count	holy mess	**quandary**
crunch	hot potato	question
dilemma	hot water	scrape
disagreement	**issue**	squeeze
dispute	mess	trouble
disputed point	nut	worriment

CURED!

*I really resent being liked openly. I don't find any **challenge** in being liked.*

JOHN CASSAVETES

Our **problem** is whether to add a new room on a tight budget or wait.

This sentence doesn't make it clear how we are viewing the problem of whether to add on the new room now or be crowded for a while longer and wait until we have more money.

powerful remedies

Substitute an alternative remedy for *problem*:

Our _____ is whether to add a new room on a tight budget or wait.

challenge	Our tight budget is certainly a difficulty, but we consider the process of figuring it out to be stimulating.
complication	We thought we had enough money for the remodel, but unexpected things happened to present a problem with the original situation.
dilemma	The need to remodel and the tight budget pose a situation requiring a choice between equally undesirable alternatives.
headache	*Headache* in this example is an informal—but clear—way of saying that not being able to reach a decision is annoying and bothersome and gives us both a need to head for the aspirin.
issue	Deciding which option is most important will determine our choice.
obstacle	The tight budget is hindering our progress, but it won't stop us from making a sound decision.
quandary	We're in a state of uncertainty about what to do, caught between equally unfavorable options.

CURED!

*The greatest **obstacle** to discovering the shape of the earth, the continents, and the oceans was not ignorance but the illusion of knowledge.*

DANIEL BOORSTIN

prove

PART OF SPEECH	*verb*
DEFINITION	*to establish the truth or genuineness of, as by evidence or argument*

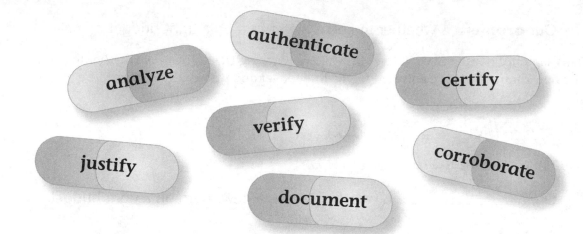

analyze · authenticate · certify · verify · justify · corroborate · document

cures for the common word

affirm
analyze
ascertain
assay
attest
authenticate
back
bear out
certify
check
confirm
convince
corroborate
declare
demonstrate

determine
document
end up
establish
evidence
evince
examine
experiment
explain
find
fix
justify
make evident
manifest
pan out

result
settle
show
substantiate
sustain
test
testify
trial
try
turn out
uphold
validate
verify
warrant
witness

CURED!

*Golfers have **analyzed** the game in order to find "the secret." There is no secret.*

HENRY COTTON

DIAGNOSIS *limiting*

The defense attorney was determined to **prove** his client's story.

Even if we assume his client is being honest, *prove* doesn't give us much information as to how the attorney will show his client's story to be true.

Substitute an alternative remedy for *prove*:

The defense attorney was determined to _____ his client's story.

analyze   The attorney is going to examine the evidence critically, to bring out the essential elements so as to identify causes and key factors.

authenticate The attorney is going to establish the story as genuine, with the help of an expert in the field.

certify   The attorney will present reliable information to attest to the truth of the story.

corroborate   The attorney has evidence, facts, or a person who can establish or strengthen his client's story.

document   The attorney will furnish specific references, citations, and so on, in support of the statements his client made.

justify   Even if his client might have broken a law, the attorney wants to show that his client's actions were just or right.

verify   The attorney will substantiate the truth of his client's story by use of a combination of evidence and testimony.

*The first thing any comedian does on getting an unscheduled laugh is to **verify** the state of his buttons.*

W. C. FIELDS

put

PART OF SPEECH   *verb*
DEFINITION   *to move or place anything into or out of a specific location or position*

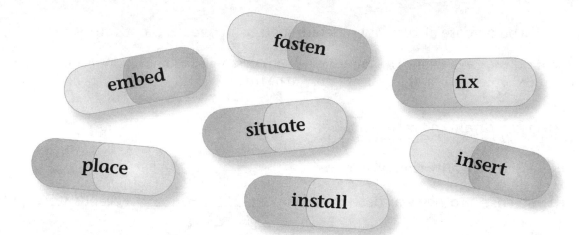

cures for the common word

bring	**insert**	plop
concenter	**install**	plunk
concentrate	invest	quarter
deposit	lay	repose
embed	nail	rest
establish	park	rivet
fasten	peg	seat
fix	**place**	settle
fixate	plank	**situate**
focus	plant	stick

CURED!

" *COFFEE.EXE missing. **Insert** cup and press any key.*

ANONYMOUS
"

Safely **put** the battery in its correct engine compartment.

We know the battery needs to be in the appropriate engine compartment but not specifically how the battery needs to be placed.

Substitute an alternative remedy for *put*:

Safely _____ the battery in its correct engine compartment.

embed   The battery needs to be placed in a compartment that completely surrounds it.

fasten   The battery needs to be attached securely to something else—like the compartment hatch.

fix   The battery needs to be stable in the compartment.

insert   The battery needs to be set into, between, or among the appropriate location in the engine compartment.

install   The battery needs to be placed in position and connected for proper use.

place   The battery needs to be put in the compartment in the proper position.

situate   We need to be sure the battery is put in the correct compartment.

CURED!

*Give me a lever long enough and a fulcrum on which to **place** it, and I shall move the world.*

ARCHIMEDES

PART OF SPEECH	*adjective*
DEFINITION	*done, proceeding, or occurring with promptness or rapidity*

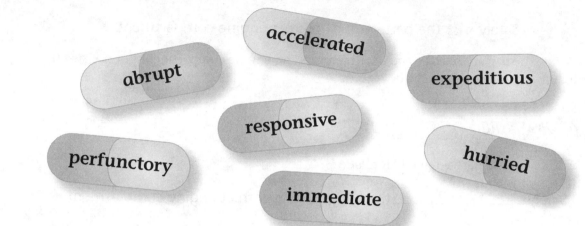

cures for the common word

abrupt	**expeditious**	**perfunctory**
accelerated	express	posthaste
active	fleet	prompt
agile	hasty	pronto
alert	headlong	rapid
animated	**hurried**	**responsive**
ASAP	**immediate**	snappy
breakneck	impatient	speedy
brief	impetuous	spirited
brisk	instantaneous	sprightly
cursory	keen	spry
curt	lively	sudden
double time	mercurial	swift
energetic	nimble	winged

*The difficult can be done **immediately**, the impossible takes a little longer.*
ARMY CORPS OF ENGINEERS

We received a **quick** response from the loan committee—"declined."

Though we're not thrilled that the answer was no, the following alternatives give a clearer indication of how we felt about the committee's decision process.

powerful remedies

Substitute an alternative remedy for *quick*:

We received a(n) _____ response from the loan committee— "declined."

abrupt
The decision was fast and also delivered in a brusque manner, as if from the surface facts, we didn't fit in a formula and they wouldn't consider us beyond the easy formula.

accelerated
The decision came in less time than required, and some of the detail to be considered might have been eliminated.

expeditious
Though the decision came with speed and efficiency, the connotation is that the facts were considered thoroughly.

hurried
We feel the committee was pushed—for some reason or by someone—to make a rapid decision and possibly did not give our request its fully due review.

immediate
The decision occurred without delay.

perfunctory
The committee made a hasty decision without thorough attention to detail.

responsive
The committee readily reacted to our appeals and efforts.

CURED!

*The **hurried** are not competent; the competent are not hurried.*
CHINESE PROVERB

quick

PART OF SPEECH   *adjective*
DEFINITION   *prompt to understand, learn, etc.*

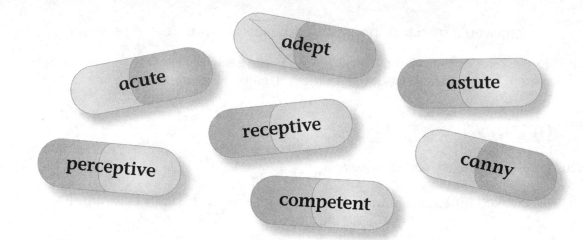

cures for the common word

able	**competent**	prompt
active	deft	quick-witted
acute	dexterous	ready
adept	discerning	**receptive**
adroit	effective	savvy
all there	effectual	sharp
apt	intelligent	shrewd
astute	keen	skillful
bright	knowing	slick
canny	nimble-witted	vigorous
capable	**perceptive**	whiz
clever	perspicacious	wise

Any event, once it has occurred, can be made to appear inevitable by a **competent** *historian.*

LEE SIMONSON

Caitlin is a **quick** learner.

She's always been fast at learning in several areas, but *quick* doesn't give us much specific information about her particular learning skills.

powerful remedies

Substitute an alternative remedy for *quick*:

Caitlin is a(n) _____ learner.

acute   Caitlin has a sharp intellect, a keen sense of perception, or both.

adept   Caitlin is very skilled in her method of learning.

astute   Caitlin is clever and observant in her learning.

canny   Caitlin shows keen and sound judgment in what and how she studies or learns.

competent   Caitlin learns adequately for whichever topic she's studying.

perceptive   Caitlin shows keen insight, understanding, or intuition about the topic she's studying.

receptive   Caitlin has a wonderful ability to easily receive knowledge, ideas, etc.

CURED!

*What helps me go forward is that I stay **receptive**, I feel that anything can happen.*

ANOUK AIMEE

ready

PART OF SPEECH	*adjective*
DEFINITION	*prepared or available for service, action, or progress*

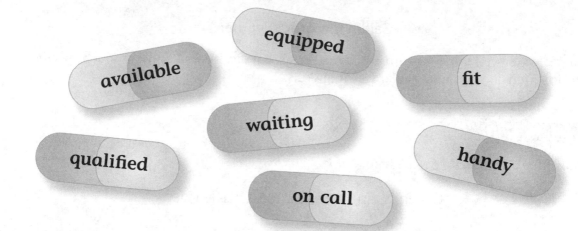

available · equipped · fit · waiting · qualified · handy · on call

cures for the common word

accessible	covered	**on call**
adjusted	**equipped**	on hand
all set	expectant	on tap
anticipating	**fit**	open to
apt	fixed for	organized
arranged	**handy**	primed
at hand	in line	**qualified**
available	in order	ripe
bagged	in place	set
completed	in position	**waiting**
convenient	near	wired

CURED!

*Television is the first truly democratic culture, the first culture **available** to everybody and entirely governed by what the people want. The most terrifying thing is what people do want.*

CLIVE BARNES

The boat is **ready** for launch.

This sentence doesn't give us clear information about the boat's readiness to launch.

powerful remedies

Substitute an alternative remedy for *ready*:

The boat is _____ for launch.

available	Perhaps it's a rental boat, and now it's ready for our use.
equipped	The boat is supplied with the necessities, such as tools or provisions.
fit	I'm glad to know the boat is in good physical condition.
handy	The boat is within easy reach or conveniently available when I am.
on call	The boat is available on short notice—all I have to do is call.
qualified	The boat has all the qualities and features required by law or custom.
waiting	The boat is remaining inactive or stationary—in anticipation of being ready when I am.

CURED!

"
*Somewhere, something incredible is **waiting** to be known.*

BLAISE PASCAL
"

regular

PART OF SPEECH · *adjective*
DEFINITION · *usual; normal; customary; recurring at fixed times; periodic*

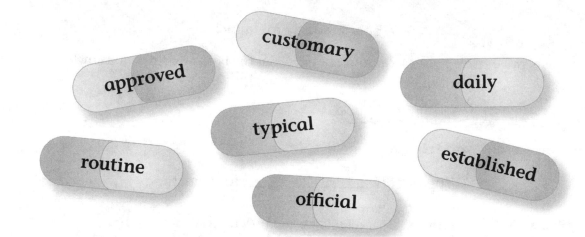

cures for the common word

approved	general	proper
bona fide	habitual	**routine**
classic	lawful	run-of-the-mill
common	legitimate	sanctioned
commonplace	natural	standard
correct	normal	time-honored
customary	**official**	traditional
daily	ordinary	**typical**
established	orthodox	unexceptional
everyday	prevailing	unvarying
formal	prevalent	usual

*It is dangerous to be right in matters on which the **established** authorities are wrong.*

FRANÇOIS-MARIE AROUET VOLTAIRE

DIAGNOSIS *vague*

The driver followed his **regular** route, despite the heavy snows.

There are several definitions for *regular*, so the alternatives tell us more precisely about the driver's route.

powerful remedies

Substitute an alternative remedy for *regular*:

The driver followed his _____ route, despite the heavy snows.

approved   The driver followed the route that was agreed to by the company he works for, his customers, or the laws—even though it isn't his preferred route.

customary   The driver followed his usual, habitual route.

daily   The driver took the same route he does every single workday.

established   The driver followed a route that is not necessarily required but conforms to accepted standards.

official   The driver took the route that was authorized and dictated by the company he works for.

routine   Like *customary*, *routine* indicates an unvarying and habitual route but with the connotation of it being unimaginative or rote procedure for the driver.

typical   The driver can take different routes, and the route he takes is representative or characteristic of the route most drivers take.

*The FBI, to its credit in a self-serving sort of way, rejects the **routine** use of the polygraph on its own people.*

ALDRICH AMES

short

PART OF SPEECH	*adjective*
DEFINITION	*abridged; brief or concise*

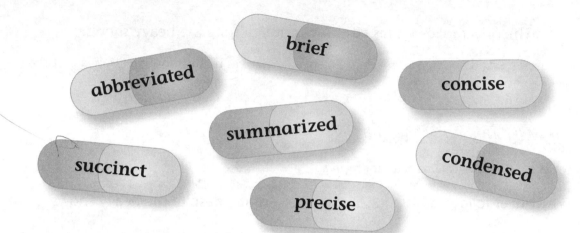

cures for the common word

abbreviated
aphoristic
bare
boiled-down
breviloquent
brief
compendiary
compendious
compressed
concise
condensed
curtailed

curtate
cut short
decreased
decurtate
diminished
epigrammatic
fleeting
laconic
lessened
little
momentary
pithy

pointed
precise
sententious
shortened
short-lived
short-term
succinct
summarized
summary
terse
undersized
unsustained

CURED!

*Vigorous writing is **concise**.*

WILLIAM STRUNK JR.

DIAGNOSIS *vague*

I had time before the meeting to read the **short** report.

We can't tell from the use of *short* if the report started out by being brief or was cut down—and if so, appropriately or not.

powerful remedies

Substitute an alternative remedy for *short*:

I had time before the meeting to read the _____ report.

abbreviated	The report has been shortened to a smaller version of the original— and we don't know if important parts of it have been omitted.
brief	The full report is of short duration.
concise	The full report is successful in being comprehensive in scope while using few words.
condensed	The report has been reduced to a shorter form but retains all the pertinent information.
precise	The report is sharply exact and accurate, though *precise* doesn't give any indication of its length.
succinct	The report is characterized by its verbal brevity, with no wasted words.
summarized	The report includes all of the primary points of a larger report, expressed in a concise form—with the connotation that none of the vital information has been lost.

CURED!

*There is no more difficult art to acquire than the art of observation, and for some men it is quite as difficult to record an observation in **brief** and plain language.*

WILLIAM OSLER

simple

PART OF SPEECH	*adjective*
DEFINITION	*clear; easy to understand, deal with, use, etc.*

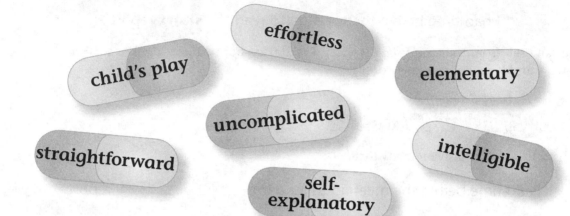

cures for the common word

child's play	manageable	snap
clean	mild	**straightforward**
easy	no problem	transparent
effortless	no sweat	**uncomplicated**
elementary	picnic	understandable
facile	plain	uninvolved
incomplex	quiet	unmistakable
intelligible	royal	unmixed
light	**self-explanatory**	untroublesome
lucid	smooth	vanilla

*Unless one is a genius, it is best to aim at being **intelligible**.*

ANTHONY HOPE

Daisy hoped the test questions would be **simple**.

In this sentence, it's not clear if Daisy might be worried that she didn't study sufficiently for the test or if her concern is based on the difficulty of the test subject itself.

powerful remedies

Substitute an alternative remedy for *simple*:

Daisy hoped the test questions would be _____.

child's play	This is an informal way to say that Daisy hopes she can easily answer the questions, because the questions are easy or because Daisy studied so well she knows the content.
effortless	Daisy hopes the questions will require no effort to answer.
elementary	Daisy hopes the questions relate to the fundamental or simplest aspects of the subject.
intelligible	Daisy hopes the questions are written in a clear way that she can easily understand.
self-explanatory	Daisy hopes that what the questions are asking for is obvious, needing no further explanation.
straightforward	Daisy hopes the questions are free from ambiguity.
uncomplicated	Daisy hopes the questions are not complex or involved.

CURED!

*Nothing so completely baffles one who is full of trick and duplicity himself, than **straightforward** and simple integrity in another.*

CHARLES CALEB COLTON

small

PART OF SPEECH   *adjective*
DEFINITION   *of limited size; of comparatively restricted dimensions; not big*

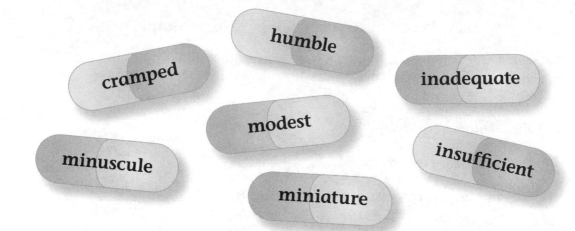

cramped   humble   inadequate   modest   minuscule   insufficient   miniature

cures for the common word

baby	microscopic	puny
bantam	mini	pygmy
bitty	**miniature**	runty
cramped	**minuscule**	scanty
diminutive	minute	short
humble	**modest**	slight
immature	narrow	small-scale
inadequate	paltry	stunted
inconsequential	petite	teeny
inconsiderable	petty	toy
insignificant	picayune	trifling
insufficient	pint-sized	trivial
limited	pitiful	undersized
little	pocket-sized	wee
meager	poor	young

CURED!

*It's hard to be **humble**, when you're as great as I am.*

MUHAMMAD ALI

The **small** house down the block is for sale.

For some, *small* would be ideal, and for others it wouldn't be, and in this sentence we're not sure whether the house being small is positive or negative.

powerful remedies

Substitute an alternative remedy for *small*:

The _____ house down the block is for sale.

cramped   The house is severely limited in space.

humble   The house is not one considered high in quality—in reference to its "rank" in relation to others in the neighborhood, as opposed to in reference to its stability.

inadequate   The house doesn't offer us enough room or other features to be suitable for the wants of our family.

insufficient   The house is lacking in what we absolutely require.

miniature   This indicates the house is a small-scale representation of a full-sized house.

minuscule   It's a very tiny house, maybe just studio sized.

modest   The house is a nice one, just free from ostentation or showy extravagance.

Nobody who takes on anything big and tough can afford to be ***modest.***
GEORGE ORSON WELLES

special

PART OF SPEECH   *adjective*
DEFINITION   *distinguished or different from what is ordinary or usual*

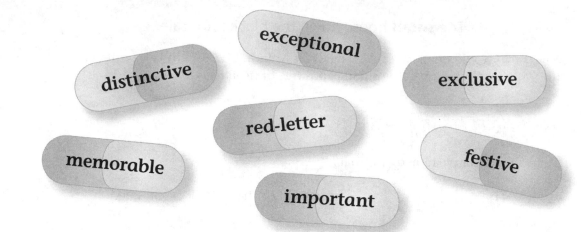

cures for the common word

certain	**festive**	primo
characteristic	first	proper
chief	gala	rare
choice	**important**	**red-letter**
defined	individual	reserved
definite	limited	restricted
designated	main	select
determinate	major	set
different	marked	significant
distinctive	**memorable**	smashing
earmarked	momentous	specialized
exceptional	particular	specific
exclusive	peculiar	uncommon
express	personal	unique
extraordinary	primary	unusual

CURED!

> *Courage is not the absence of fear, but rather the judgement that something else is more **important** than fear.*
>
> AMBROSE REDMOON

John and Tawni want to plan a **special** day together.

Special implies that John and Tawni are planning a wonderful day, but it doesn't tell us enough about in what way it will not be a typical day.

powerful remedies

Substitute an alternative remedy for *special*:

John and Tawni want to plan a(n) _____ _____ day together.

distinctive   They want the day to have a unique and different quality, implying in a positive way.

exceptional   They are planning something for their day that will be a rare instance and/or unusually excellent.

exclusive   The connotation is that they want a day together alone—omitting anyone else from their plans.

festive   They are planning a day that's joyous, full of fun and gaiety.

important   They want to do something of great significance to them both.

memorable   It will be a day worth remembering.

red-letter   This is an informal way to say it will be a memorable day that is especially important or happy for them.

*Good design is making something intelligible and **memorable**. Great design is making something memorable and meaningful.*

DIETER RAMS

stay

PART OF SPEECH	*verb*
DEFINITION	*to spend some time in a place, in a situation, with a person or group, etc.*

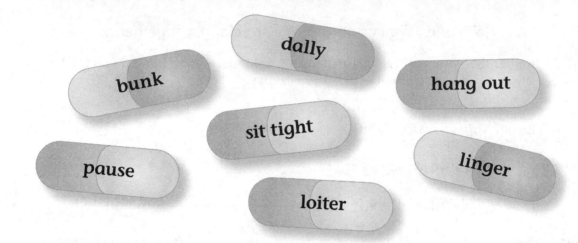

cures for the common word

abide	**hang out**	respite
bide	hover	roost
bunk	lag	settle
continue	last	**sit tight**
dally	**linger**	sojourn
delay	**loiter**	squat
dillydally	nest	stand
endure	outstay	stay out
establish oneself	**pause**	stay put
halt	perch	stick around
hang	procrastinate	stop
hang about	remain	sweat
hang around	reprieve	sweat it
hang in	reside	tarry

"
*Now and then it's good to **pause** in our pursuit of happiness and just be happy.*

GUILLAUME APOLLINAIRE
"

DIAGNOSIS   *vague*

Bert wanted to **stay** at Ernie's house after school.

This sentence doesn't tell us much about why and for how long Bert wants to stay at Ernie's house.

powerful remedies

Substitute an alternative remedy for *stay*:

Bert wanted to _____ at Ernie's house after school.

bunk   Bert wants to sleep over at Ernie's.

dally   Bert may be having fun, but choosing *dally* means to waste time, so maybe he's supposed to be doing homework or chores.

hang out Bert wants to spend time at Ernie's because he likes Ernie and the things they do there.

linger   Bert is reluctant to leave, so he's staying longer than expected.

loiter   Bert is lingering aimlessly at Ernie's—and Ernie isn't even home.

pause   Bert just wanted to stop for a short time at Ernie's on his way home.

sit tight This is a slang expression meaning Bert has decided to stay at Ernie's for a while, biding his time and taking no action.

*Why hurry over beautiful things? Why not **linger** and enjoy them?*
CLARA SCHUMANN

strange

PART OF SPEECH	*adjective*
DEFINITION	*deviating; unusual, extraordinary, or curious; odd*

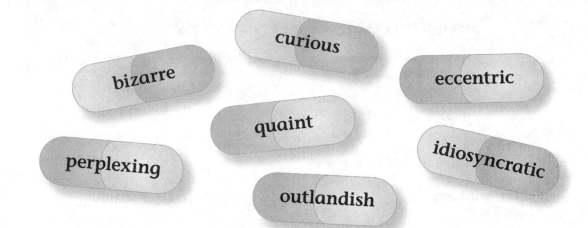

cures for the common word

aberrant	**idiosyncratic**	**perplexing**
abnormal	ignorant	**quaint**
astonishing	inexperienced	queer
astounding	irregular	rare
atypical	marvelous	remarkable
bizarre	mystifying	singular
curious	new	unaccountable
different	newfangled	unaccustomed
eccentric	odd	uncanny
erratic	oddball	uncommon
exceptional	off	unfamiliar
extraordinary	offbeat	unheard of
fantastic	**outlandish**	unseasoned
far-out	out-of-the-way	unusual
funny	peculiar	weird

CURED!

*Middle Age is that **perplexing** time of life when we hear two voices calling us, one saying, "Why not?" and the other, "Why bother?"*

SYDNEY J. HARRIS

DIAGNOSIS *vague*

The man's **strange** clothes made him stand out.

There are a lot of different types of clothes that could be considered strange, partially determined by the viewer, and *strange* in this sentence doesn't indicate what about the man's clothes made him stand out.

Substitute an alternative remedy for *strange*:

The man's _____ clothes made him stand out.

bizarre	His clothing was markedly unusual in appearance—in fact, outrageously or whimsically odd.
curious	His clothes aroused attention, being inexplicable or highly unusual—for example, a football uniform as he walked his dog.
eccentric	His way of dressing deviated from the conventional—for example, a top hat with his workout clothes.
idiosyncratic	Though we don't have a clue as to why he's dressing that way, it likely makes perfect sense to him.
outlandish	His clothing was freakishly odd in appearance, but the connotation is that it is simply wildly inappropriate for the occasion.
perplexing	His clothing is confusing—for example, wearing a heavy wool coat on a hot and sunny day.
quaint	His clothing has an old-fashioned attractiveness or charm and is oddly picturesque in a pleasing or amusing way.

Eccentric behavior is not routinely noticed around a movie set.

GENE TIERNEY

take

PART OF SPEECH   *verb*

DEFINITION   *to get into one's hold or possession by voluntary action or by force, skill, or artifice*

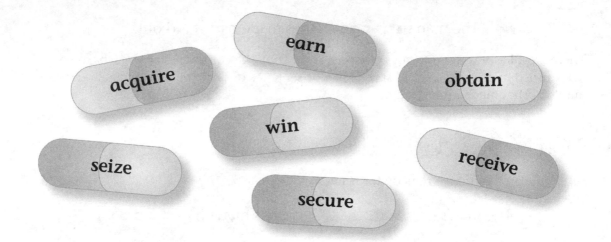

cures for the common word

abduct	**earn**	**obtain**
accept	ensnare	overtake
acquire	entrap	pick up
arrest	gain possession	pull in
attain	gather up	reach
bag	glom	reap
capture	grab	**receive**
carry off	grasp	**secure**
carve out	grip	**seize**
catch	handle	select
choose	haul in	snag
clasp	have	snatch
clutch	hold	strike
collar	nab	take in
collect	nail	**win**

Happiness is like those palaces in fairy tales . . . we must fight in order to ***obtain*** *it.*

ALEXANDRE DUMAS

> The investors will **take** control of the company next week.

Though *take* often has a very neutral meaning—neither positive or negative—in this sentence it gives the sense that the takeover may have been hostile; whereas, the following alternatives give us a truer picture.

powerful remedies

Substitute an alternative remedy for *take*:

> The investors will _____ control of the company next week.

acquire	The investors will come into possession or ownership of the company, possibly simply by purchase.
earn	The investors will deservedly have control.
obtain	The investors will come into possession of the company either through their efforts or by a request.
receive	Possession of the company was offered to the investors—most likely for a price or an exchange of some kind—and the investors have agreed.
secure	The investors thought they would be taking control, and now they will be able to ensure this.
seize	The investors have found a way to take possession by force; the connotation is that it may happen in an underhanded and partially secretive way.
win	The investors will gain control through their labor or through a successful competition, such as winning a bidding war for the company.

CURED!

*What a child doesn't **receive** he can seldom later give.*

P. D. JAMES

take

PART OF SPEECH *verb*
DEFINITION *to accept, handle, or deal with in a particular way; to endure*

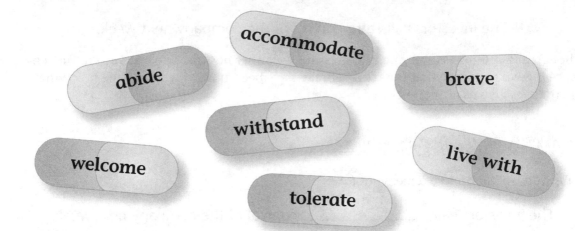

cures for the common word

abide	hack	stand for
accept	hang in	stomach
accommodate	hang on	submit to
bear	hang tough	suffer
bear with	hold	swallow
brave	let in	take it
brook	**live with**	**tolerate**
contain	lump it	undergo
give access	receive	weather
go	ride out	**welcome**
go through	stand	**withstand**

*I respect those who resist me; but I cannot **tolerate** them.*

CHARLES DEGAULLE

> My boyfriend can **take** the cold weather much better than I can.

We can't tell from this use of *take* much about his attitude toward cold weather—if he loves the cold or just puts up with it.

##

Substitute an alternative remedy for *take*:

> My boyfriend can _____ the cold weather much better than I can.

abide
He can tolerate and withstand the cold without yielding or submitting to freezing or to finding a way to get warm.

accommodate
He manages to adapt to make being cold suitable for him.

brave
He faces the cold courageously.

live with
He can accept the cold weather perhaps as a trade-off for other advantages that go with a cold-weather climate.

tolerate
He can endure the cold without even being upset by being cold.

welcome
He actually accepts the cold with pleasure.

withstand
He successfully resists and endures the cold, whereas I just have to find a fireplace or a heater.

CURED!

*Fortune favors the **brave**.*

VIRGIL

thin

PART OF SPEECH   *adjective*
DEFINITION   *of relatively slight consistency; scant; not abundant or plentiful*

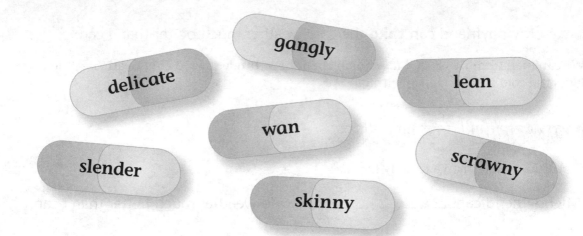

cures for the common word

attenuated	lightweight	**slender**
beanpole	meager	slight
bony	narrow	slim
cadaverous	peaked	small
delicate	pinched	spare
emaciated	puny	spindly
ethereal	rangy	starved
featherweight	rarefied	subtle
fine	rawboned	threadlike
fragile	reedy	twiggy
gangly	rickety	undernourished
gaunt	**scrawny**	underweight
haggard	shriveled	**wan**
lanky	skeletal	wasted
lean	**skinny**	wizened

*A wise child pleases his father; a **skinny** dog shames his master.*

CHINESE PROVERB

DIAGNOSIS *vague*

As a teenager, Nicole was always **thin**.

Thin can very easily have either positive or negative connotations, so we want to be more specific—and perhaps more "gentle" when describing Nicole's appearance.

Substitute an alternative remedy for *thin*:

As a teenager, Nicole was always _____.

delicate	Nicole had such a slight build that she looked fragile and might easily be susceptible to illness.
gangly	Nicole was awkwardly tall and spindly.
lean	Nicole didn't have much fat and looks healthy.
scrawny	Nicole was so excessively thin, she looked like she was starving.
skinny	*Skinny* is a less-than-flattering way of saying that Nicole is thin.
slender	Nicole's slight figure gave the impression of her being light and graceful.
wan	Nicole's weight gave her the appearance of being ill, fatigued, and even unhappy.

CURED!

"The **delicate** and infirm go for sympathy, not to the well and buoyant, but to those who have suffered like themselves.

CATHERINE E. BEECHER

think

PART OF SPEECH	verb
DEFINITION	to contemplate; to employ one's mind rationally and objectively

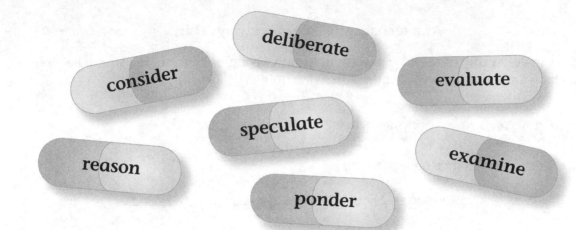

cures for the common word

analyze
appraise
appreciate
brood
cerebrate
chew
cogitate
comprehend
conceive
consider
deduce
deliberate
estimate

evaluate
examine
figure out
ideate
imagine
infer
intellectualize
judge
logicalize
meditate
mull
mull over
muse

noodle
ponder
rationalize
reason
reflect
resolve
ruminate
sort out
speculate
stew
study
turn over
weigh

*When in charge, **ponder**. When in trouble, delegate. When in doubt, mumble.*

SOLWAY COMMUNITY PRESS

Think long and hard about the consequences before you quit school.

Good advice, though choosing *think* for this sentence doesn't tell us how carefully and thoroughly you're considering the consequences.

Substitute an alternative remedy for *think*:

_____ long and hard about the consequences before you quit school.

consider	It's important to reflect carefully about the decision you're about to make; the connotation is that you're taking the situation seriously.
deliberate	You will think carefully and slowly about the choice to be made and may consult with another or others in the process of reaching a decision.
evaluate	You're judging the significance, worth, or quality of your decision.
examine	You're taking time to carefully inspect, scrutinize, and investigate the possible sequences.
ponder	You're considering your decision deeply and thoroughly.
reason	You are aiming to form conclusions based on the facts you know.
speculate	You're casually talking over the consequences conjecturally without sufficient reason to reach a conclusion.

" *I don't **consider** myself bald, I'm just taller than my hair.*

TOM SHARPE "

PART OF SPEECH	*verb*
DEFINITION	*to attempt to do or accomplish*

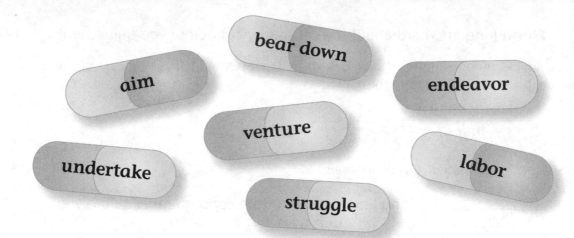

cures for the common word

aim	**endeavor**	shoot for
aspire	essay	speculate
attack	exert oneself	strive
attempt	go after	**struggle**
bear down	hump it	tackle
buckle down	**labor**	**undertake**
compete	lay to	**venture**
contend	propose	vie for
contest	risk	work
drive for	seek	wrangle

CURED!

> *Let us **endeavor** to live, so that when we die, even the undertaker will be sorry.*
>
> MARK TWAIN

DIAGNOSIS *vague*

I'm going to **try** to learn French before our family vacation.

Try doesn't indicate the strength of my commitment or say how hard I'm going to try or how successful I think I'll be.

powerful remedies

Substitute an alternative remedy for *try*:

I'm going to _____ to learn French before our family vacation.

aim	The key point is that I'm directing my efforts to learning *before* our vacation.
bear down	I'm going to work harder than I have in the past to learn, intensifying my efforts.
endeavor	I'm going to dedicate real effort in attempting to learn, but the implication is that I feel I may not be completely successful.
labor	I'm going to work hard toward my goal of learning French.
struggle	I'll be strenuously engaged in what I consider the problem of learning French.
undertake	I'm going to take it upon myself to learn French for all of us, maybe because they've left it to me to be the family translator.
venture	I'm going to work to learn French, even if some of my friends doubt I'll be successful.

*In the **struggle** between the stone and the water, in time, the water wins.*
CHINESE PROVERB

use

PART OF SPEECH	*verb*
DEFINITION	*to employ for some purpose; to put into service*

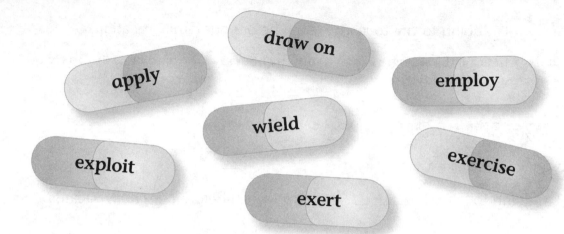

apply · draw on · employ · wield · exploit · exercise · exert

cures for the common word

accept	exhaust	ply
adopt	expend	practice
apply	**exploit**	put forth
bestow	govern	regulate
capitalize	handle	relate
consume	make do	run
control	make use	run through
do with	make with	spend
draw on	manage	utilize
employ	manipulate	waste
exercise	operate	**wield**
exert	play on	work

CURED!

*Under Capitalism, man **exploits** man. Under Communism, it's exactly the opposite.*

JOHN KENNETH GALBRAITH

DIAGNOSIS *vague*

Mr. and Mrs. Doors **use** their influence when fund-raising.

We'd like to think their influence is used in a good way, but we can't be sure in this sentence, whereas the alternatives tell us more about their intentions.

powerful remedies

Substitute an alternative remedy for *use*:

Mr. and Mrs. Doors _____ their influence when fund-raising.

apply	Their intention is to use their influence in a positive way when engaging with potential donors, though *apply* can have somewhat of a negative connotation.
draw on	They consider their influence a source to encourage donors—perhaps offering something in exchange for donations.
employ	They consider their influence a tool to achieve their goal.
exercise	They are putting their influence to use to have a desired effect.
exert	The implication when choosing *exert* is that they may be using their influence to try to force donors to contribute.
exploit	There's no doubt when choosing *exploit* that they are using their influence selfishly for their own ends.
wield	It's for a good cause, but they're exercising their power in a dominating way.

*The less people know about what is really going on, the easier it is to **wield** power and authority.*

CHARLES, PRINCE OF WALES

usual

PART OF SPEECH   *adjective*
DEFINITION   *commonplace; everyday*

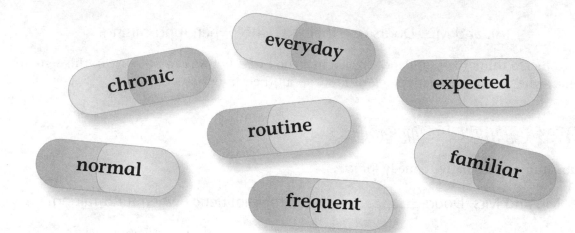

everyday

chronic

expected

routine

normal

familiar

frequent

cures for the common word

accepted
accustomed
average
chronic
commonplace
constant
conventional
current
customary
everyday
expected
familiar
fixed

frequent
garden variety
general
grind
groove
habitual
mainstream
matter-of-course
natural
normal
ordinary
plain
prevailing

prevalent
quotidian
regular
rife
routine
so-so
standard
stock
typical
unremarkable
vanilla
wonted
workaday

CURED!

*Romance is the glamour which turns the dust of **everyday** life into a golden haze.*

ELINOR GLYN

We discussed the **usual** problems at the meeting.

There's no way to tell from the use of *usual* in this sentence whether the problems are new or recurring, daunting or manageable.

Substitute an alternative remedy for *usual*:

We discussed the _____ problems at the meeting.

chronic   They are continuing and recurring problems we've been discussing for a long time.

everyday   They are problems that occur on a very regular basis.

expected   They are problems we considered were likely or probable to occur.

familiar   They are problems that are commonly known or seen.

frequent   They are problems that occur either quite often or at close intervals.

normal   The problems are the standard or common type.

routine   The problems either are ordinary and unvarying or are often repeated.

*No one realizes how beautiful it is to travel until he comes home and rests his head on his old, **familiar** pillow.*

LIN YUTANG

want

PART OF SPEECH	*verb*
DEFINITION	*to feel a need or a desire for; to wish for*

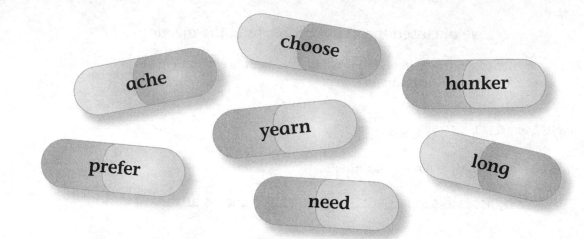

cures for the common word

ache	fancy	**need**
aspire	**hanker**	pine
be greedy	have ambition	**prefer**
choose	hunger	require
covet	incline toward	spoil for
crave	itch for	thirst
cream for	lech for	wish
desiderate	**long**	**yearn**
die over	lust	yen for

*The last of the human freedoms is to **choose** one's attitude in any given set of circumstances.*

VIKTOR E. FRANKL

I **want** to get away from all computers and phones this weekend.

It's time for a break from technology, but *want* doesn't give a clear enough idea of the degree of my get-away urgency.

powerful remedies

Substitute an alternative remedy for *want*:

I _____ to get away from all computers and phones this weekend.

ache	I'm very eager to get away; in fact, the thought of not getting away is painful.
choose	I have a number of possibilities for what to do this weekend, and I pick getting away.
hanker	I have a restless longing to get away.
long	I have a heartfelt desire, stronger than hoping, to get away, but for this weekend, it's probably beyond my reach.
need	This is beyond a wish—I require relief!
prefer	If given a choice for this weekend, I'd select going away.
yearn	I have such a strong and earnest desire to get away, I'm practically dreaming of it.

*After four years at the United Nations I sometimes **yearn** for the peace and tranquillity of a political convention.*

ADLAI E. STEVENSON

weird

PART OF SPEECH	*adjective*
DEFINITION	*of a strikingly odd or unusual character, strange*

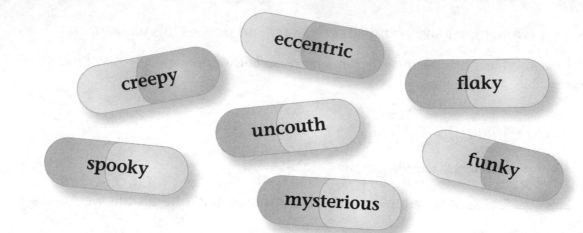

cures for the common word

awful	grotesque	peculiar
creepy	haunting	preternatural
curious	horrific	queer
dreadful	kinky	secret
eccentric	kooky	singular
eerie	magical	**spooky**
far-out	**mysterious**	strange
flaky	occult	supernatural
freaky	odd	uncanny
funky	oddball	**uncouth**
ghastly	ominous	unearthly
ghostly	outlandish	unnatural

*That so few now dare to be **eccentric** marks the chief danger of the time.*

JOHN STUART MILL

DIAGNOSIS *vague*

I just met my **weird** new neighbors.

We know *weird* indicates that the neighbors are out of the ordinary, but we're not sure in what way or if *weird* here means they're good, bad, or neither—just different.

powerful remedies

Substitute an alternative remedy for *weird*:

I just met my _____ new neighbors.

creepy   My neighbors give me a sensation of uneasiness or fear or seem annoyingly unpleasant.

eccentric   The neighbors' behavior is a bit odd and unconventional, departing from an established "norm."

flaky   My neighbors are nice enough but not very reliable.

funky   They're unconventional but in a modish, humorous, tongue-in-cheek way.

mysterious There's something about the neighbors that seems to elude explanation, leaving me wondering and wanting to find out more.

spooky   Ooh, these people are a little scary.

uncouth   My neighbors' habits are unrefined, to say the least.

CURED!

*The most beautiful thing we can experience is the **mysterious**. It is the source of all art and science.*

ALBERT EINSTEIN

well

PART OF SPEECH	*adverb*
DEFINITION	*in a good, proper, commendable, or satisfactory manner; excellently; skillfully*

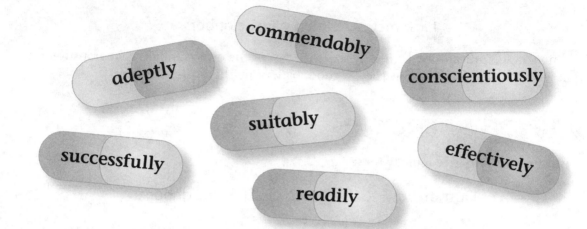

cures for the common word

ably	**conscientiously**	profoundly
accurately	correctly	properly
adeptly	**effectively**	**readily**
adequately	efficiently	rightly
admirably	effortlessly	satisfactorily
agreeably	excellently	skillfully
attentively	expertly	smoothly
capably	famously	soundly
capitally	favorably	splendidly
carefully	fully	strongly
closely	irreproachably	**successfully**
commendably	nicely	**suitably**
competently	pleasantly	thoroughly
completely	proficiently	with skill

*People will accept your ideas much more **readily** if you tell them Benjamin Franklin said it first.*

DAVID H. COMINS

For a few months, the conservatives and the liberals worked
well together.

Though it's clearly a positive way they were working together, *well* doesn't tell us what we consider good about this accomplishment, nor does it tell us much about what made their cooperation possible.

powerful remedies

Substitute an alternative remedy for *well*:

For a few months, the conservatives and the liberals worked
_____ together.

adeptly	They worked together in a very skilled and expert manner.
commendably	They worked together in a way worthy of special praise.
conscientiously	Guided by and in accordance with the dictates of their consciences, they worked in a principled way.
effectively	They worked together adequately to accomplish the intended or expected result—but probably not much beyond that.
readily	They actually worked together willingly.
successfully	They worked together to a favorable outcome.
suitably	They worked in an appropriate and fitting way.

CURED!

*The genius of a good leader is to leave behind him a situation which common sense, without the grace of genius, can deal with **successfully**.*

WALTER LIPPMANN

Minicapsules

absolutely ADVERB 6

positively; certainly; having no restriction, exception, or qualification

actually, categorically, completely, **conclusively**, **consummately**, **decidedly**, decisively, def, definitely, doubtless, **easily**, entirely, exactly, **fully**, ideally, positively, **precisely**, purely, really, right on, straight out, sure enough, surely, thoroughly, truly, unambiguously, **unconditionally**, unquestionably, utterly, wholly

activity NOUN 8

a specific deed, action, or function

act, avocation, bag, ball game, bit, deed, endeavor, **enterprise**, entertainment, **exercise**, game, hobby, interest, **job**, labor, occupation, **pastime**, **project**, **pursuit**, racket, scene, scheme, stunt, **task**, undertaking, venture, work

affect VERB 10

to produce a material influence upon or alteration in

act on, **alter**, change, disturb, impinge, impress, incline, induce, **influence**, inspire, interest, involve, moderate, **modify**, motivate, move, overcome, perturb, prevail, **prompt**, regard, relate, stir, **sway**, touch, **transform**, **upset**

amazing ADJECTIVE 12

causing great surprise or sudden wonder

affecting, **alarming**, astonishing, astounding, **bewildering**, blown away, bowled down, bowled over, dazing, dazzling, **dumbfounding**, **electrifying**, flabbergasting, **impressive**, moving, overwhelming, perplexing, put away, **remarkable**, **shocking**, staggering, startling, striking, stunning, stupefying, touching, unexpected

awesome ADJECTIVE 14

very impressive; inspiring; terrific, extraordinary

alarming, astonishing, **awe-inspiring**, awful, beautiful, **breathtaking**, daunting, dreadful, exalted, fabulous, fearful, fearsome, formidable, frantic, frightening, grand, horrifying, **imposing**, **impressive**, intimidating, magnificent, **majestic**, mind-blowing, **moving**, nervous, outstanding, overwhelming, shocking, striking, stunning, stupefying, stupendous, terrible, terrifying, wonderful, **wondrous**

bad ADJECTIVE 16

of poor or inferior quality; defective; deficient

abominable, amiss, **atrocious**, awful, bad news, beastly, bottom out, bummer, careless, **cheap**, corrupt, crummy, **defective**, deficient, disagreeable, dissatisfactory, dreadful, erroneous, fallacious, faulty, harmful, imperfect, inadequate, incorrect, **inferior**, injurious, lousy, off, **offensive**, poor, repulsive, rough, sad, skuzzy, **sleazy**, **slipshod**, stinking, substandard, synthetic, unacceptable, unfavorable, unsatisfactory

basic ADJECTIVE 18

elementary; of, being, or serving as a starting point; fundamental

basal, beginning, capital, central, **chief**, easy, elemental, **elementary**, **essential**, **foundational**, fundamental, indispensable, inherent, intrinsic, **introductory**, **key**, main, necessary, primary, primitive, **principal**, radical, rudimentary, simplified, substratal, underlying, vital

beautiful ADJECTIVE 20

having qualities that give great pleasure or satisfaction to see, hear, think about; delighting the senses or mind

alluring, **angelic**, appealing, attractive, beauteous, bewitching, charming, classy, comely, cute, dazzling, **delicate**, delightful, divine, **elegant**, enticing, excellent, exquisite, fair, **fascinating**, fine, foxy, good-looking, gorgeous, **graceful**, grand, handsome, ideal, lovely, magnificent, marvelous, pleasing, pretty, radiant, ravishing, refined, resplendent, shapely, splendid, statuesque, **stunning**, sublime, superb, taking, wonderful

begin VERB 22

to perform the first or earliest part of some action; to commence; to start

activate, actualize, break ground, bring about, cause, **commence**, create, effect, **embark on**, enter on, enter upon, establish, eventuate, found, generate, get going, give impulse, go ahead, go into, impel, inaugurate, induce, **initiate**, instigate, institute, introduce, **launch**, lead, make, make active, motivate, **mount**, occasion, open, originate, **plunge into**, prepare, produce, set about, set up, trigger, **undertake**

better ADJECTIVE 24

greater in excellence or higher in quality

bigger, choice, exceeding, **exceptional**, finer, fitter, greater, **higher quality**, improved, larger, **more appropriate**, more desirable, more fitting, more select, more suitable, more useful, more valuable, **preferable**, preferred, prominent, **sophisticated**, **superior**, surpassing, **worthier**

big ADJECTIVE 26

large, as in size, height, width, or amount

ample, brimming, bulky, burly, capacious, chock-full, **colossal**, commodious, considerable, copious, enormous, **extensive**, fat, full, gigantic, heavy-duty, heavyweight, **hefty**, huge, hulking, humungous, husky, immense, jumbo, king-sized, mammoth, **massive**, monster, oversize, ponderous, **prodigious**, roomy, sizable, spacious, strapping, stuffed, **substantial**, thundering, vast, voluminous, walloping, **whopping**

boring ADJECTIVE 28

uninteresting and tiresome; dull

bomb, bromidic, characterless, colorless, commonplace, drab, drag, drudging, dull, flat, ho-hum, humdrum, insipid, **interminable**, irksome, lifeless, **monotonous**, platitudinous, plebeian, prosaic, repetitious, routine, spiritless, **stale**, stereotypical, **stodgy**, stuffy, stupid, tame, **tedious**, threadbare, tiresome, tiring, trite, **unexciting**, vapid, **wearisome**, well-worn, zero

bring VERB 30

to carry, convey, lead, or cause to go along to another place

accompany, attend, back, bear, carry, **chaperone**, companion, conduct, consort, convey, deliver, **escort**, fetch, gather, guide, heel, hump, import, **lead**, lug, pack, pick up, piggyback, ride, **schlepp**, shoulder, take, take along, tote, transfer, **transport**, truck, **usher**

certain ADJECTIVE 32

confident; free from doubt or reservation

absolute, **assured**, believing, calm, clear, **conclusive**, convinced, definite, **evident**, firm, **fixed**, guaranteed, incontrovertible, indubitable, infallible, **irrefutable**, known, plain, positive, predestined, real, **reliable**, safe, sanguine, secure, set, sound, sure, true, **unambiguous**, undeniable, unequivocal, unerring, unmistakable, unquestionable, verifiable

change VERB 34

to make different from what it is or from what it would be if left alone

accommodate, **adapt**, **adjust**, alter, alternate, commute, convert, **diminish**, diverge, diversify, evolve, fluctuate, make innovations, make over, **moderate**, **modify**, modulate, mutate, naturalize, recondition, redo, reform, regenerate, remake, remodel, renovate, **reorganize**, replace, resolve, restyle, revolutionize, shape, shift, substitute, tamper with, transfigure, transform, translate, transmute, transpose, turn, vacillate, **vary**, veer, warp

choose VERB 36

to select from a number of possible alternatives; to decide on and pick out

accept, adopt, appoint, cast, co-opt, crave, cull, decide on, designate, desire, determine, **elect**, **embrace**, excerpt, extract, fancy, **favor**, finger, fix on, glean, **identify**, judge, love, name, **nominate**, opt for, predestine, **prefer**, see fit, select, set aside, settle upon, sift out, single out, slot, sort, tag, take, tap, want, weigh, will, winnow, wish, wish for

common ADJECTIVE 38

ordinary; widespread; general; of frequent occurrence; usual; familiar

accepted, average, banal, bourgeois, casual, characteristic, colloquial, **conventional**, current, customary, daily, everyday, **familiar**, frequent, general, habitual, hackneyed, homely, humdrum, informal, **mediocre**, monotonous, natural, obscure, passable, plain, prevailing, prevalent, prosaic, regular, **routine**, run-of-the-mill, **simple**, **stale**, standard, stereotypical, **stock**, trite, typical, undistinguished, universal, unvaried, usual, wearisome, workaday

correct ADJECTIVE 40

free from error; especially conforming to fact or truth

actual, amen, **appropriate**, equitable, exact, **factual**, faithful, faultless, flawless, for sure, impeccable, just, **legitimate**, nice, OK, **on target**, perfect, **precise**, **proper**, regular, right, righteous, rigorous, stone, strict, true, **undistorted**, unmistaken, veracious, veridical

correct VERB 42

to set or make true, accurate, or right; to remove the errors or faults from

alter, ameliorate, amend, better, change, **clean up**, cure, debug, do over, doctor, **edit**, emend, fiddle with, fix up, go over, help, improve, launder, make over, make right, mend, pay dues, pick up, **polish**, reclaim, reconstruct, rectify, redress, reform, regulate, remedy, remodel, **reorganize**, repair, retouch, **review**, **revise**, right, set right, set straight, shape up, straighten out, **touch up**, turn around, upgrade

decent ADJECTIVE 44

respectable; suitable; conforming to a recognized standard of good taste

adequate, **appropriate**, approved, **becoming**, befitting, **chaste**, clean, comely, conforming, continent, correct, decorous, delicate, ethical, fair, fit, fitting, good, honest, honorable, **immaculate**, mannerly, modest, moral, nice, noble, presentable, **proper**, prudent, pure, reserved, **respectable**, right, spotless, stainless, standard, straight, **suitable**, trustworthy, unblemished, undefiled, untarnished, upright, virtuous, worthy

develop VERB 46

to bring out the capabilities or possibilities of; to cause to grow or expand

actualize, advance, amplify, **augment**, beautify, broaden, build up, cultivate, deepen, dilate, elaborate, enlarge, **enrich**, evolve, exploit, extend, finish, heighten, **improve**, intensify, **lengthen**, magnify, materialize, **perfect**, polish, promote, realize, **refine**, **strengthen**, stretch, unfold, widen, work out

difficult ADJECTIVE 48

not easily or readily done

ambitious, **arduous**, **backbreaking**, bothersome, burdensome, **challenging**, crucial, **demanding**, effortful, exacting, formidable, galling, gargantuan, hard, hard-won, heavy, **herculean**, immense, **intricate**, irritating, labored, **laborious**, onerous, painful, problem, problematic, prohibitive, rigid, severe, strenuous, titanic, toilsome, tough, troublesome, trying, unyielding, uphill, upstream, wearisome

difficult ADJECTIVE 50

complicated; hard to comprehend

abstract, abstruse, baffling, bewildering, **complex**, confounding, confusing, dark, deep, delicate, **enigmatic**, enigmatical, **entangled**, esoteric, formidable, hard, hidden, inexplicable, intricate, involved, knotty, labyrinthine, loose, meandering, **mysterious**, mystifying, obscure, obstinate, paradoxical, **perplexing**, **problematical**, profound, puzzling, rambling, subtle, tangled, **thorny**, ticklish, troublesome, unclear, unfathomable, unintelligible

direct ADJECTIVE 52

honest; straightforward; frank; candid

absolute, bald, **blunt**, **candid**, categorical, downright, **explicit**, express, **forthright**, frank, genuine, guileless, matter-of-fact, open, **outspoken**, plain, plain-spoken, point-blank, sincere, straight, straightforward, truthful, **unambiguous**, unconcealed, undisguised, **unequivocal**, unreserved

do VERB 54

to perform, execute, carry out

accomplish, achieve, act, **arrange**, bring about, cause, complete, conclude, cook, **create**, determine, discharge, effect, end, engage in, **execute**, finish, fix, fulfill, get ready, look after, make, make ready, move, operate, **organize**, perform, perk, **prepare**, **produce**, pull off, see to, succeed, take on, transact, **undertake**, wind up, work, wrap up

easy ADJECTIVE 56

capable of being accomplished or acquired with ease; posing no difficulty

accessible, apparent, basic, child's play, cinch, clear, comfortable, **effortless**, **elementary**, evident, facile, inconsiderable, light, little, **manageable**, manifest, mere, natural, no bother, no problem, no sweat, no trouble, **obvious**, **painless**, paltry, picnic, plain, plain sailing, pleasant, pushover, relaxed, royal, simple, slight, smooth, snap, straightforward, **uncomplicated**, undemanding, uninvolved, untroublesome, yielding

effective ADJECTIVE 58

producing the intended or expected result; adequate to accomplish a purpose

able, active, adequate, capable, cogent, **compelling**, competent, **convincing**, direct, effectual, efficacious, **efficient**, emphatic, energetic, **forceful**, forcible, impressive, live, moving, operative, **persuasive**, potent, **powerful**, powerhouse, **practical**, producing, resultant, serviceable, serving, sound, striking, successful, sufficient, telling, trenchant, useful, valid, virtuous, yielding

emphasize VERB 60

to lay stress upon; to single out as important

accent, **accentuate**, affirm, **articulate**, assert, charge, **dramatize**, enlarge, enunciate, headline, **highlight**, impress, indicate, insist on, italicize, maintain, make clear, mark, pinpoint, play up, point out, press, prioritize, pronounce, punctuate, **reiterate**, repeat, rub in, spot, **spotlight**, underline, **underscore**, weight

end VERB 62

to come to a conclusion; to terminate or cease

abolish, abort, accomplish, achieve, **break off**, break up, call off, cease, close, close out, complete, **conclude**, consummate, crown, culminate, cut short, **delay**, determine, discontinue, dispose of, dissolve, drop, expire, **finish**, get done, give up, halt, **interrupt**, perorate, **postpone**, quit, relinquish, **resolve**, settle, sew up, shut down, stop, terminate, ultimate, wind up, wrap, wrap up

energy NOUN 64

the capacity for vigorous activity; abundant available power

animation, ardor, birr, dash, **drive**, dynamism, élan, **endurance**, enterprise, exertion, fire, force, forcefulness, fortitude, get-up-and-go, go, initiative, **intensity**, juice, life, **liveliness**, might, moxie, muscle, pep, **pizzazz**, pluck, potency, power, puissance, punch, spirit, spontaneity, **stamina**, steam, strength, toughness, tuck, vehemence, verve, vigor, vim, vitality, **zeal**, zest

enjoy VERB 66

to experience joy or satisfaction from; to take pleasure in

adore, **appreciate**, be entertained, be pleased, **delight in**, dig, dote on, drink in, eat up, fancy, flip for, flip over, funk, go, groove on, have fun, like, **love**, **luxuriate in**, mind, pleasure in, rejoice in, **relish**, revel in, **savor**, savvy, take to

enough ADJECTIVE 68

adequate for the want or need; sufficient for the purpose or to satisfy desire

abundant, acceptable, **adequate**, **ample**, bellyful, bounteous, bountiful, comfortable, competent, complete, **copious**, decent, fed up, full, had it, last straw, lavish, plenteous, **plentiful**, replete, satisfactory, satisfying, **sufficient**, sufficing, **suitable**, tolerable, **unlimited**

excellent ADJECTIVE 70

of the highest or finest quality; exceptionally good of its kind

accomplished, admirable, attractive, champion, choice, desirable, distinctive, **distinguished**, estimable, exceptional, **exemplary**, exquisite, fine, first, first-class, first-rate, good, great, high, **incomparable**, **invaluable**, magnificent, meritorious, **notable**, noted, outstanding, peerless, premium, priceless, prime, remarkable, select, **skillful**, splendid, sterling, striking, superb, superior, superlative, supreme, **tiptop**, top-notch, transcendent, unsurpassed, wonderful

exciting ADJECTIVE 72

producing excitement or strong feeling in; stirring; thrilling; exhilarating

animating, appealing, arousing, **arresting**, **astonishing**, bracing, breathtaking, dangerous, **dramatic**, **electrifying**, exhilarant, eye-popping, far-out, fine, flashy, heady, hectic, impelling, impressive, interesting, **intoxicating**, intriguing, lively, melodramatic, mind-blowing, moving, neat, overpowering, overwhelming, **provocative**, racy, rip-roaring, rousing, sensational, showy, spine-tingling, stimulating, **stirring**, thrilling, titillating, wild, zestful

fast ADJECTIVE 74

quick; swift; moving or able to move, operate, function, or take effect quickly

accelerated, active, **agile**, breakneck, **brisk**, chop-chop, **dashing**, double time, electric, **expeditious**, expeditive, flashing, fleet, fleeting, flying, hair-trigger, **hasty**, hot, hurried, hypersonic, instant, lickety-split, like crazy, mercurial, **nimble**, PDQ, posthaste, presto, pronto, quick, racing, rapid, ready, screamin', snap, snappy, **swift**, velocious, winged

feel VERB 76

to perceive or examine by touch

caress, clasp, **clutch**, explore, finger, fondle, frisk, **fumble**, grapple, grasp, grip, **grope**, **handle**, manipulate, maul, palm, palpate, paw, perceive, pinch, ply, poke, press, **sense**, **squeeze**, stroke, test, thumb, tickle, **touch**, try, twiddle, wield

fill VERB 78

to occupy to the full capacity

block, brim over, bulge out, charge, choke, **clog**, close, congest, **cram**, crowd, distend, fulfill, furnish, glut, gorge, heap, impregnate, inflate, jam-pack, lade, load, meet, occupy, overflow, **pack**, permeate, pervade, plug, pump up, ram, replenish, sate, satiate, satisfy, **saturate**, shoal, **stock**, store, stretch, stuff, suffuse, **supply**, swell, take up, **top off**

final ADJECTIVE 80

conclusive or decisive; coming to the end; last in place, order, or time

absolute, **bottom-line**, **closing**, **concluding**, crowning, decided, decisive, definite, definitive, determinate, determinative, ending, **eventual**, finished, finishing, hindmost, incontrovertible, irrefutable, **irrevocable**, **last-minute**, latest, latter, settled, supreme, swan song, terminal, terminating, **ultimate**, unanswerable, unappealable

fine ADJECTIVE 82

of superior or best quality; excellent

accomplished, aces, **admirable**, attractive, beautiful, capital, choice, dandy, **elegant**, exceptional, expensive, exquisite, **fashionable**, first-class, **first-rate**, five-star, good-looking, great, handsome, lovely, magnificent, ornate, outstanding, pleasant, rare, **refined**, select, showy, skillful, **smart**, spiffy, splendid, **striking**, subtle, superior, supreme, top-notch, well-made, wicked

finish VERB 84

to get done

accomplish, achieve, bag it, **break up**, carry through, cease, chuck, clinch, close, complete, conclude, consume, cool it, crown, culminate, deplete, determine, discharge, end, execute, exhaust, **finalize**, fold, fulfill, **halt**, make, mop up, perfect, round off, scratch, **scrub**, settle, sew up, **shut down**, shutter, stop, terminate, wrap, **wrap up**

funny ADJECTIVE 86

humorous; causing amusement or laughter; comical

absurd, **amusing**, antic, a scream, **bizarre**, blithe, capricious, **clever**, comical, diverting, droll, entertaining, facetious, farcical, gay, good-humored, hilarious, humorous, **hysterical**, jocular, joking, jolly, killing, knee-slapping, laughable, **ludicrous**, merry, mirthful, playful, priceless, rich, ridiculous, riotous, risible, side-splitting, silly, slapstick, sportive, uncommon, unusual, **whimsical**, **witty**

get VERB 88

to come into possession or use of; to acquire as a result of action or effort

access, accomplish, achieve, acquire, annex, attain, bag, build up, buy out, **capture**, clean up, come by, cop, draw, earn, educe, **elicit**, evoke, extort, **extract**, fetch, **gain**, **glean**, grab, inherit, land, lock up, make, net, obtain, parlay, pick up, **procure**, pull, rack up, realize, reap, receive, score, **secure**, snag, snap up, take, wangle, win

give VERB 90

to impart or communicate

accord, **administer**, ante up, award, bequeath, **bestow**, cede, commit, **confer**, consign, convey, deed, deliver, dish out, **dispense**, distribute, **dole out**, donate, endow, entrust, fork over, furnish, grant, hand, **impart**, lease, let have, parcel out, part with, pass out, permit, pony up, present, **provide**, relinquish, remit, sell, shell out, subsidize, supply, throw in, transfer, transmit, vouchsafe, will

go VERB 92

to move or proceed, especially to or from something

abscond, advance, approach, beat it, bug out, **cruise**, decamp, depart, **escape**, exit, fare, flee, fly, **get away**, get going, **hie**, hightail, **journey**, lam, leave, light out, mosey, move, pass, **proceed**, progress, pull out, push on, quit, repair, **retire**, run away, shove off, skip out, split, take flight, take off, tool, travel, vamoose, wend, withdraw

good ADJECTIVE 94

pleasant; enjoyable

acceptable, ace, admirable, agreeable, bully, capital, choice, **commendable**, competent, congenial, deluxe, excellent, exceptional, favorable, first-class, functional, **gratifying**, great, **honorable**, marvelous, nice, pleasing, positive, precious, prime, reputable, **satisfying**, select, serviceable, shipshape, sound, spanking, splendid, sterling, stupendous, super, superb, superior, tip-top, **valuable**, **welcome**, **wonderful**

good ADJECTIVE 96

having the qualities that are desirable or distinguishing in a particular thing; skilled

able, **accomplished**, adept, adroit, au fait, capable, clever, competent, dexterous, efficient, **experienced**, expert, first-rate, **masterful**, proficient, proper, qualified, reliable, **responsible**, satisfactory, serviceable, **skillful**, suitable, suited, **talented**, thorough, trained, **trustworthy**, useful, wicked

great ADJECTIVE 98

important; eminent; distinguished; remarkable or outstanding

august, capital, celebrated, chief, **commanding**, dignified, **distinguished**, eminent, exalted, excellent, famous, glorious, grand, **heroic**, **highly regarded**, honorable, **idealistic**, illustrious, impressive, leading, lofty, lordly, **magnanimous**, major, noble, notable, noted, outstanding, paramount, primary, principal, prominent, puissant, regal, remarkable, renowned, royal, stately, sublime, superior, superlative, **talented**

grow VERB 100

to expand or increase gradually by concerted effort

abound, **advance**, age, amplify, arise, augment, breed, **build**, **burgeon**, cultivate, **develop**, dilate, enlarge, **expand**, extend, fill out, **flourish**, gain, germinate, heighten, increase, issue, luxuriate, maturate, **mature**, mount, multiply, originate, produce, propagate, pullulate, raise, ripen, rise, shoot, spread, sprout, stem, stretch, swell, thicken, thrive, turn, wax, widen

happy ADJECTIVE 102

enjoying or showing joy or pleasure or good fortune

blessed, blissful, blithe, captivated, **cheerful**, chipper, content, convivial, delighted, **delightful**, ecstatic, elated, exultant, flying high, gay, glad, gleeful, gratified, hopped up, intoxicated, jolly, joyous, jubilant, laughing, light, **lively**, merry, **mirthful**, overjoyed, **peaceful**, peppy, perky, **playful**, pleasant, pleased, satisfied, sparkling, sunny, thrilled, tickled pink, up, **upbeat**

hard ADJECTIVE 104

difficult to do or accomplish; fatiguing; troublesome

arduous, backbreaking, ball-breaking, bothersome, burdensome, complex, **complicated**, **demanding**, distressing, exacting, **exhausting**, fatiguing, **formidable**, grinding, hairy, harsh, heavy, herculean, intricate, involved, irksome, knotty, laborious, mean, merciless, murderous, onerous, operose, rigorous, rough, **rugged**, scabrous, serious, severe, slavish, sticky, **strenuous**, terrible, tiring, toilsome, tough, troublesome, unsparing, wearing, wearisome

help VERB 106

to give aid; to be of service or advantage; to assist

abet, accommodate, advocate, aid, **assist**, back, ballyhoo, **befriend**, benefit, **bolster**, boost, buck up, cheer, cooperate, **encourage**, endorse, further, intercede, maintain, open doors, patronize, plug, promote, prop, puff, push, relieve, root for, sanction, save, second, serve, **stand by**, stimulate, stump for, succor, **support**, **sustain**, uphold

important ADJECTIVE 108

substantial; of much or great significance or consequence

big-league, chief, considerable, conspicuous, critical, crucial, decisive, earnest, **essential**, exceptional, exigent, extensive, far-reaching, foremost, front-page, grave, great, heavy, **imperative**, importunate, **influential**, large, marked, material, **meaningful**, momentous, notable, of note, of substance, **paramount**, ponderous, pressing, primary, principal, **relevant**, salient, serious, signal, **significant**, something, standout, substantial, urgent, vital, weighty

interesting ADJECTIVE 110

arousing the curiosity or engaging the attention

absorbing, affecting, alluring, **amusing**, arresting, captivating, charismatic, **compelling**, curious, delightful, elegant, enchanting, engaging, engrossing, entertaining, enthralling, entrancing, exceptional, exotic, **fascinating**, gracious, gripping, impressive, inspiring, **intriguing**, inviting, magnetic, pleasing, pleasurable, provocative, refreshing, **riveting**, **stimulating**, stirring, striking, suspicious, thought-provoking, unusual, winning

keep VERB 112

to hold or retain in one's possession

accumulate, **amass**, cache, care for, carry, conduct, conserve, control, **deposit**, detain, direct, enjoy, garner, grasp, grip, have, **heap**, hold back, **maintain**, manage, own, pile, place, possess, preserve, put up, reserve, retain, **save**, stack, stock, **store**, withhold

kind ADJECTIVE 114

of a good or benevolent nature or disposition

affectionate, all heart, altruistic, **amiable**, amicable, beneficent, benevolent, big, bounteous, charitable, clement **compassionate**, congenial, considerate, cordial, courteous, **friendly**, **generous**, gentle, good-hearted, gracious, humane, humanitarian, **indulgent**, kindhearted, kindly, lenient, loving, mild, neighborly, **obliging**, philanthropic, propitious, softhearted, sympathetic, tenderhearted, thoughtful, tolerant, understanding

know VERB 116

to perceive or understand as fact or truth; to apprehend clearly and with certainty

apperceive, **appreciate**, apprehend, be acquainted, be cognizant, be informed, be read, be versed, cognize, **comprehend**, differentiate, **discern**, discriminate, distinguish, experience, **fathom**, feel certain, grasp, have, **ken**, **learn**, **notice**, perceive, realize, recognize, see, understand

leave VERB 118

to depart from permanently; to quit

abandon, abscond, break away, cast off, clear out, cut out, decamp, defect, **desert**, disappear, **ditch**, embark, emigrate, **escape**, **exit**, **flee**, flit, fly, **forsake**, go away, go forth, head out, migrate, move out, part, pull out, push off, quit, relinquish, retire, ride off, run along, sally, scram, set out, slip out, split, step down, take leave, take off, vacate, vamoose, vanish, walk out, withdraw

look NOUN 120

the way in which a person or thing appears to the eye or to the mind

air, aspect, attitude, **bearing**, cast, character, complexion, **countenance**, **demeanor**, **effect**, expression, face, fashion, feature, form, guise, image, **manner**, **mien**, mug, physiognomy, posture, presence, seeming, semblance, shape, visage

love NOUN 122

a profoundly tender, passionate affection for another person or an object

adulation, **affection**, allegiance, amity, amour, **appreciation**, ardor, attachment, crush, delight, **devotion**, emotion, enchantment, enjoyment, fervor, fidelity, fondness, friendship, hankering, idolatry, inclination, **infatuation**, involvement, liking, **lust**, partiality, passion, rapture, **regard**, relish, respect, sentiment, soft spot, taste, tenderness, weakness, **worship**, yearning, zeal

main ADJECTIVE 124

chief in size, extent, or importance; principal; leading

capital, cardinal, central, chief, controlling, critical, crucial, **dominant**, essential, first, **foremost**, **fundamental**, head, **leading**, major, **necessary**, **outstanding**, paramount, particular, predominant, preeminent, premier, prevailing, primary, prime, special, star, stellar, supreme, **vital**

make VERB 126

to cause to exist or happen; to bring about; to create

accomplish, adjust, **arrange**, **assemble**, beget, brew, **bring about**, **build**, cause, compile, compose, conceive, constitute, construct, cook up, dream up, effect, engender, fabricate, fashion, father, forge, form, frame, generate, hatch, initiate, **invent**, knock out, manufacture, mold, occasion, originate, parent, **prepare**, procreate, produce, put together, secure, shape, sire, spawn, synthesize, **throw together**, whip up

mean ADJECTIVE 128

hostile, offensive, selfish, or unaccommodating; nasty; malicious

bad-tempered, bitchy, callous, **cantankerous**, **churlish**, contemptible, **dangerous**, despicable, difficult, dirty, disagreeable, **dishonorable**, **evil**, **formidable**, hard, hard-nosed, ignoble, ill-tempered, infamous, knavish, liverish, lousy, malicious, malign, nasty, perfidious, pesky, rotten, rough, rude, rugged, scurrilous, shameless, sinking, snide, sour, the lowest, treacherous, **troublesome**, ugly, unfriendly, unpleasant, unscrupulous, vexatious, vicious

more ADJECTIVE 130

additional or further; in greater quantity, amount, measure, degree, or number

added, additional, amassed, another, augmented, bounteous, **deeper**, enhanced, exceeding, **expanded**, extended, extra, farther, **fresh**, further, greater, **heavier**, higher, increased, innumerable, larger, likewise, **major**, massed, new, numerous, other, replenishment, **supplementary**, **wider**

need NOUN 132

urgent want, as of something required or wanted

ache, charge, **commitment**, committal, **compulsion**, craving, demand, desire, devoir, **duty**, exigency, extremity, hunger, itch, **longing**, must, **obligation**, occasion, requirement, requisite, right, thirst, urge, **urgency**, use, weakness, **wish**

new ADJECTIVE 134

of recent origin, production, purchase, etc.

dewy, different, dissimilar, distinct, edgy, fashionable, **fresh**, inexperienced, just out, **latest**, **modern**, modernistic, modish, neoteric, newfangled, **novel**, now, original, recent, strange, topical, ultramodern, uncontaminated, **unfamiliar**, **unique**, unknown, unlike, unseasoned, unskilled, unspoiled, untouched, untrained, **untried**, untrodden, unused, unusual, up-to-date, virgin, youthful

next ADJECTIVE 136

immediately following in time, order, importance, etc.

abutting, **adjacent**, **adjoining**, after, alongside, attached, beside, bordering, close, **closest**, coming, connecting, consecutive, consequent, contiguous, ensuing, **following**, immediate, later, nearby, **nearest**, **neighboring**, proximate, **subsequent**, succeeding, thereafter, touching

nice ADJECTIVE 138

pleasing and agreeable in nature

admirable, agreeable, amiable, approved, attractive, **becoming**, **charming**, commendable, considerate, copacetic, **cordial**, courteous, **cultured**, decorous, delightful, favorable, friendly, genial, **gentle**, good, **gracious**, helpful, hunky-dory, ingratiating, inviting, kind, kindly, lovely, nifty, obliging, OK, peachy, pleasant, pleasurable, polite, seemly, swell, unpresumptuous, welcome, **well-mannered**, winning, winsome

old ADJECTIVE 140

having lived or existed for a relatively long time; far advanced in years or life

aged, ancient, broken down, debilitated, decrepit, deficient, doddering, elderly, enfeebled, exhausted, **experienced**, fossil, geriatric, getting on, gray-haired, grizzled, hoary, impaired, inactive, infirm, **mature**, matured, olden, patriarchal, **seasoned**, senile, **senior**, **skilled**, superannuated, tired, used, venerable, versed, **veteran**, wasted, worn

old ADJECTIVE 142

obsolete; no longer in general use

aboriginal, age-old, antediluvian, **antiquated**, antique, archaic, bygone, cast-off, crumbling, dated, decayed, démodéd, early, erstwhile, **former**, hackneyed, immemorial, late, moth-eaten, of yore, olden, oldfangled, **old-fashioned**, old-time, **onetime**, **original**, outdated, outmoded, passé, past, previous, primeval, **primitive**, primordial, quondam, remote, rusty, stale, superannuated, time-worn, traditional, unfashionable, unoriginal, venerable, **worn-out**

open ADJECTIVE 144

not closed or barred; relatively free of obstructions

accessible, agape, **airy**, ajar, bare, clear, cleared, dehiscent, disclosed, emptied, expansive, **exposed**, extended, free, gaping, naked, **navigable**, patent, patulous, peeled, revealed, rolling, **spacious**, spread out, stripped, susceptible, unbarred, unblocked, unbolted, unburdened, **uncluttered**, uncovered, unfolded, unfurled, unimpeded, unlocked, **unobstructed**, unsealed, unstopped, vacated, wide, yawning

part NOUN 146

a portion or division of a whole that is separate or distinct

allotment, apportionment, articulation, bit, branch, chunk, component, constituent, department, detail, division, element, factor, **fraction**, **fragment**, helping, hunk, ingredient, installment, item, limb, lot, measure, member, module, moiety, molecule, organ, **parcel**, particle, piece, portion, quantum, **ration**, scrap, section, **sector**, **segment**, share, side, slice, sliver, splinter, subdivision, unit

perfect ADJECTIVE 148

entirely without any flaws, defects, or shortcomings

absolute, **accomplished**, aces, adept, beyond compare, blameless, **classical**, **consummate**, crowning, culminating, defectless, excellent, excelling, **experienced**, expert, faultless, finished, flawless, foolproof, ideal, immaculate, **impeccable**, indefectible, masterful, masterly, matchless, paradisiacal, peerless, pure, skilled, skillful, **sound**, splendid, spotless, stainless, sublime, superb, supreme, ten, unblemished, **unequaled**, unmarred, untainted, untarnished, utopian

piece NOUN 150

a separate or limited portion or quantity of something

allotment, bit, **bite**, case, chomp, chunk, cut, division, example, fraction, fragment, **gob**, half, hunk, instance, interest, item, length, lot, **lump**, member, moiety, **morsel**, mouthful, parcel, percentage, portion, quantity, quota, sample, **scrap**, section, segment, share, shred, **slice**, smithereens, snack, specimen

plain ADJECTIVE 152

straightforward; frank or candid

abrupt, artless, blunt, candid, direct, downright, **forthright**, frank, genuine, **guileless**, **honest**, impolite, **ingenuous**, open, **outspoken**, rude, **sincere**, straight arrow, straightforward, true, unconcealed, undisguised, **unfeigned**, uninhibited, unreserved, unrestricted, unvarnished

plan NOUN 154

a scheme or method of acting, doing, proceeding, making, etc.

aim, **angle**, animus, arrangement, big picture, contrivance, deal, design, device, disposition, expedient, **game plan**, **gimmick**, idea, intendment, intention, layout, machination, means, **method**, outline, pattern, picture, **platform**, plot, policy, procedure, program, project, proposal, proposition, purpose, scenario, scheme, **stratagem**, **strategy**, suggestion, system, tactic, treatment, undertaking, way

plan VERB 156

to think out; to arrange a method or scheme to accomplish an objective

arrange, bargain for, block out, blueprint, brainstorm, calculate, concoct, conspire, contemplate, contrive, cook up, **craft**, design, **devise**, draft, **engineer**, figure out, fix to, form, **formulate**, frame, hatch, intrigue, invent, line up, map, **mastermind**, meditate, organize, **outline**, plot, prepare, project, quarterback, ready, reckon on, represent, rough in, scheme, set out, **shape**, sketch, steer, trace, work out

pleasant ADJECTIVE 158

socially acceptable or adept; polite; amiable; agreeable

affable, agreeable, amiable, amusing, bland, charming, **cheerful**, cheery, civilized, **congenial**, convivial, copacetic, cordial, delightful, **diplomatic**, enchanting, **engaging**, enjoyable, fine, friendly, fun, genial, genteel, good-humored, gracious, gratifying, jolly, jovial, kindly, likable, lovely, mild-mannered, nice, obliging, pleasing, pleasurable, **polite**, refreshing, satisfying, social, soft, sweet, **sympathetic**, urbane, welcome

problem NOUN 160

situation, matter, or person that presents perplexity or difficulty

box, **challenge**, **complication**, count, crunch, **dilemma**, disagreement, dispute, disputed point, doubt, **headache**, hitch, holy mess, hot potato, hot water, **issue**, mess, nut, **obstacle**, pickle, predicament, **quandary**, question, scrape, squeeze, trouble, worriment

prove VERB 162

to establish the truth or genuineness of, as by evidence or argument

affirm, **analyze**, ascertain, assay, attest, **authenticate**, back, bear out, **certify**, check, confirm, convince, **corroborate**, declare, demonstrate, determine, **document**, end up, establish, evidence, evince, examine, experiment, explain, find, fix, **justify**, make evident, manifest, pan out, result, settle, show, substantiate, sustain, test, testify, trial, try, turn out, uphold, validate, **verify**, warrant, witness

put VERB 164

to move or place anything into or out of a specific location or position

bring, concenter, concentrate, deposit, **embed**, establish, **fasten**, **fix**, fixate, focus, **insert**, **install**, invest, lay, nail, park, peg, **place**, plank, plant, plop, plunk, quarter, repose, rest, rivet, seat, settle, **situate**, stick

quick ADJECTIVE 166

done, proceeding, or occurring with promptness or rapidity

abrupt, **accelerated**, active, agile, alert, animated, ASAP, breakneck, brief, brisk, cursory, curt, double time, energetic, **expeditious**, expeditive, express, fleet, flying, harefooted, hasty, headlong, **hurried**, **immediate**, impatient, impetuous, instantaneous, keen, lively, mercurial, nimble, **perfunctory**, posthaste, prompt, pronto, rapid, **responsive**, snappy, speedy, spirited, sprightly, spry, sudden, swift, winged

quick ADJECTIVE 168

prompt to understand, learn, etc.

able, active, **acute**, **adept**, adroit, all there, apt, **astute**, bright, **canny**, capable, clever, **competent**, deft, dexterous, discerning, effective, effectual, intelligent, keen, knowing, nimble-witted, **perceptive**, perspicacious, prompt, quick-witted, ready, **receptive**, savvy, sharp, shrewd, skillful, slick, vigorous, whiz, wise

ready ADJECTIVE 170

prepared or available for service, action, or progress

accessible, adjusted, all set, anticipating, apt, arranged, at hand, **available**, bagged, completed, convenient, covered, **equipped**, expectant, **fit**, fixed for, **handy**, in line, in order, in place, in position, near, **on call**, on hand, on tap, open to, organized, primed, **qualified**, ripe, set, **waiting**, wired

regular ADJECTIVE 172

usual; normal; customary; recurring at fixed times; periodic

approved, bona fide, classic, common, commonplace, correct, **customary**, **daily**, **established**, everyday, formal, general, habitual, lawful, legitimate, natural, normal, **official**, ordinary, orthodox, prevailing, prevalent, proper, **routine**, run-of-the-mill, sanctioned, standard, time-honored, traditional, **typical**, unexceptional, unvarying, usual

short ADJECTIVE 174

abridged; brief or concise

abbreviated, aphoristic, bare, boiled-down, breviloquent, **brief**, compendiary, compendious, compressed, **concise**, **condensed**, curtailed, curtate, cut short, decreased, decurtate, diminished, epigrammatic, fleeting, laconic, lessened, little, momentary, pithy, pointed, **precise**, sententious, shortened, short-lived, short-term, **succinct**, **summarized**, summary, terse, undersized, unsustained

simple ADJECTIVE 176

clear; easy to understand, deal with, use, etc.

child's play, clean, easy, **effortless**, **elementary**, facile, incomplex, **intelligible**, light, lucid, manageable, mild, no problem, no sweat, picnic, plain, quiet, royal, **self-explanatory**, smooth, snap, **straightforward**, transparent, **uncomplicated**, understandable, uninvolved, unmistakable, unmixed, untroublesome, vanilla

small ADJECTIVE 178

of limited size; of comparatively restricted dimensions; not big

baby, bantam, bitty, **cramped**, diminutive, **humble**, immature, **inadequate**, inconsequential, inconsiderable, insignificant, **insufficient**, limited, little, meager, microscopic, mini, **miniature**, **minuscule**, minute, **modest**, narrow, paltry, petite, petty, picayune, pint-sized, pitiful, pocket-sized, poor, puny, pygmy, runty, scanty, short, slight, small-scale, stunted, teeny, toy, trifling, trivial, undersized, wee, young

special ADJECTIVE 180

distinguished or different from what is ordinary or usual

certain, characteristic, chief, choice, defined, definite, designated, determinate, different, **distinctive**, earmarked, **exceptional**, **exclusive**, express, extraordinary, **festive**, first, gala, **important**, individual, limited, main, major, marked, **memorable**, momentous, particular, peculiar, personal, primary, primo, proper, rare, **red-letter**, reserved, restricted, select, set, significant, smashing, specialized, specific, uncommon, unique, unusual

stay VERB 182

to spend some time in a place, in a situation, with a person or group, etc.

abide, bide, **bunk**, continue, **dally**, delay, dillydally, endure, establish oneself, halt, hang, hang about, hang around, hang in, **hang out**, hover, lag, last, **linger**, **loiter**, nest, outstay, **pause**, perch, procrastinate, remain, reprieve, reside, respite, roost, settle, **sit tight**, sojourn, squat, stand, stay out, stay put, stick around, stop, sweat, sweat it, tarry

strange ADJECTIVE 184

deviating; unusual, extraordinary, or curious; odd

aberrant, abnormal, astonishing, astounding, atypical, **bizarre**, **curious**, different, **eccentric**, erratic, exceptional, extraordinary, fantastic, far-out, funny, **idiosyncratic**, ignorant, inexperienced, irregular, marvelous, mystifying, new, newfangled, odd, oddball, off, offbeat, **outlandish**, out-of-the-way, peculiar, **perplexing**, **quaint**, queer, rare, remarkable, singular, unaccountable, unaccustomed, uncanny, uncommon, unfamiliar, unheard of, unseasoned, unusual, weird

take VERB 186

to get into one's hold or possession by voluntary action or by force, skill, or artifice

abduct, accept, **acquire**, arrest, attain, bag, capture, carry off, carve out, catch, choose, clasp, clutch, collar, collect, **earn**, ensnare, entrap, gain possession, gather up, glom, grab, grasp, grip, handle, haul in, have, hold, nab, nail, **obtain**, overtake, pick up, pull in, reach, reap, **receive**, **secure**, **seize**, select, snag, snatch, strike, take in, **win**

take VERB 188

to accept, handle, or deal with in a particular way; to endure

abide, accept, **accommodate**, bear, bear with, **brave**, brook, contain, give access, go, go through, hack, hang in, hang on, hang tough, hold, let in, **live with**, lump it, receive, ride out, stand, stand for, stomach, submit to, suffer, swallow, take it, **tolerate**, undergo, weather, **welcome**, **withstand**

thin ADJECTIVE 190

of relatively slight consistency; scant; not abundant or plentiful

attenuated, beanpole, bony, cadaverous, **delicate**, emaciated, ethereal, featherweight, fine, fragile, **gangly**, gaunt, haggard, lanky, **lean**, lightweight, meager, narrow, peaked, pinched, puny, rangy, rarefied, rawboned, reedy, rickety, **scrawny**, shriveled, skeletal, **skinny**, **slender**, slight, slim, small, spare, spindly, starved, subtle, threadlike, twiggy, undernourished, underweight, **wan**, wasted, wizened

think VERB 192

to contemplate; to employ one's mind rationally and objectively

analyze, appraise, appreciate, brood, cerebrate, chew, cogitate, comprehend, conceive, **consider**, deduce, **deliberate**, estimate, **evaluate**, **examine**, figure out, ideate, imagine, infer, intellectualize, judge, logicalize, meditate, mull, mull over, muse, noodle, **ponder**, rationalize, **reason**, reflect, resolve, ruminate, sort out, **speculate**, stew, study, turn over, weigh

try VERB 194

to attempt to do or accomplish

aim, aspire, attack, attempt, **bear down**, buckle down, compete, contend, contest, drive for, **endeavor**, essay, exert oneself, go after, hump it, **labor**, lay to, propose, risk, seek, shoot for, speculate, strive, **struggle**, tackle, **undertake**, **venture**, vie for, work, wrangle

use VERB 196

to employ for some purpose; put into service

accept, adopt, **apply**, bestow, capitalize, consume, control, do with, **draw on**, **employ**, **exercise**, **exert**, exhaust, expend, **exploit**, govern, handle, make do, make use, make with, manage, manipulate, operate, play on, ply, practice, put forth, regulate, relate, run, run through, spend, utilize, waste, **wield**, work

usual ADJECTIVE 198

commonplace; everyday

accepted, accustomed, average, **chronic**, commonplace, constant, conventional, current, customary, **everyday**, **expected**, **familiar**, fixed, **frequent**, garden variety, general, grind, groove, habitual, mainstream, matter-of-course, natural, **normal**, ordinary, plain, prevailing, prevalent, quotidian, regular, rife, **routine**, so-so, standard, stock, typical, unremarkable, vanilla, wonted, workaday

want VERB 200

to feel a need or a desire for; wish for

ache, aspire, be greedy, **choose**, covet, crave, cream for, desiderate, die over, fancy, **hanker**, have ambition, hunger, incline toward, itch for, lech for, **long**, lust, **need**, pine, **prefer**, require, spoil for, thirst, wish, **yearn**, yen for

weird ADJECTIVE 198

of a strikingly odd or unusual character, strange

awful, **creepy**, curious, dreadful, **eccentric**, eerie, far-out, **flaky**, freaky, **funky**, ghastly, ghostly, grotesque, haunting, horrific, kinky, kooky, magical, **mysterious**, occult, odd, oddball, ominous, outlandish, peculiar, preternatural, queer, secret, singular, **spooky**, strange, supernatural, uncanny, **uncouth**, unearthly, unnatural

well ADVERB 200

in a good, proper, commendable, or satisfactory manner; excellently; skillfully

ably, accurately, **adeptly**, adequately, admirably, agreeably, attentively, capably, capitally, carefully, closely, **commendably**, competently, completely, **conscientiously**, correctly, **effectively**, efficiently, effortlessly, excellently, expertly, famously, favorably, fully, irreproachably, nicely, pleasantly, proficiently, profoundly, properly, **readily**, rightly, satisfactorily, skillfully, smoothly, soundly, splendidly, strongly, **successfully**, **suitably**, thoroughly, with skill